The Trial of Andrew Robinson Bowes, Esq. Edward Lucas, Francis Peacock, Mark Prevot, John Cummins, otherwise called Charles Chapman, William Pigg, John Bickley, Henry Bourn, and Thomas Bowes, Attorney at Law, on Wednesday, the 30th Day of May, 1787, in...

E. Hodgson

The Trial of Andrew Robinson Bowes, Esq. Edward Lucas, Francis Peacock, Mark Prevot,
John Cummins, otherwise called Charles Chapman, William Pigg, John Bickley, Henry Bourn,
and Thomas Bowes, Attorney at Law, on Wednesday, the 30th Day of May, 1787, in hi

The Making of Modern Law collection of legal archives constitutes a genuine revolution in historical legal research because it opens up a wealth of rare and previously inaccessible sources in legal, constitutional, administrative, political, cultural, intellectual, and social history. This unique collection consists of three extensive archives that provide insight into more than 300 years of American and British history. These collections include:

Legal Treatises, 1800-1926: over 20,000 legal treatises provide a comprehensive collection in legal history, business and economics, politics and government.

Trials, 1600-1926: nearly 10,000 titles reveal the drama of famous, infamous, and obscure courtroom cases in America and the British Empire across three centuries.

Primary Sources, 1620-1926: includes reports, statutes and regulations in American history, including early state codes, municipal ordinances, constitutional conventions and compilations, and law dictionaries.

These archives provide a unique research tool for tracking the development of our modern legal system and how it has affected our culture, government, business – nearly every aspect of our everyday life. For the first time, these high-quality digital scans of original works are available via print-on-demand, making them readily accessible to libraries, students, independent scholars, and readers of all ages.

The BiblioLife Network

This project was made possible in part by the BiblioLife Network (BLN), a project aimed at addressing some of the huge challenges facing book preservationists around the world. The BLN includes libraries, library networks, archives, subject matter experts, online communities and library service providers. We believe every book ever published should be available as a high-quality print reproduction; printed on-demand anywhere in the world. This insures the ongoing accessibility of the content and helps generate sustainable revenue for the libraries and organizations that work to preserve these important materials.

The following book is in the "public domain" and represents an authentic reproduction of the text as printed by the original publisher. While we have attempted to accurately maintain the integrity of the original work, there are sometimes problems with the original work or the micro-film from which the books were digitized. This can result in minor errors in reproduction. Possible imperfections include missing and blurred pages, poor pictures, markings and other reproduction issues beyond our control. Because this work is culturally important, we have made it available as part of our commitment to protecting, preserving, and promoting the world's literature.

GUIDE TO FOLD-OUTS MAPS and OVERSIZED IMAGES

The book you are reading was digitized from microfilm captured over the past thirty to forty years. Years after the creation of the original microfilm, the book was converted to digital files and made available in an online database.

In an online database, page images do not need to conform to the size restrictions found in a printed book. When converting these images back into a printed bound book, the page sizes are standardized in ways that maintain the detail of the original. For large images, such as fold-out maps, the original page image is split into two or more pages

Guidelines used to determine how to split the page image follows:

• Some images are split vertically; large images require vertical and horizontal splits.
• For horizontal splits, the content is split left to right.
• For vertical splits, the content is split from top to bottom.
• For both vertical and horizontal splits, the image is processed from top left to bottom right.

THE

TRIAL

OF

ANDREW ROBINSON BOWES, Esq.
EDWARD LUCAS, FRANCIS PEACOCK, MARK PRE-
VOT, JOHN CUMMINS, otherwife called CHARLES CHAP-
MAN, WILLIAM PIGG, JOHN BICKLEY, HENRY
BOURN, and THOMAS BOWES, Attorney at Law;

FOR A

CONSPIRACY, &c.

PRICE THREE SHILLINGS AND SIXPENCE.

THE

TRIAL

OF

ANDREW ROBINSON BOWES, Esq.

EDWARD LUCAS, FRANCIS PEACOCK, MARK PREVOT, JOHN CUMMINS, otherwise called CHARLES CHAPMAN, WILLIAM PIGG, JOHN BICKLEY, HENRY BOURN, and THOMAS BOWES, Attorney at Law,

ON

WEDNESDAY, the 30th Day of MAY, 1787,

IN HIS

MAJESTY's COURT OF KING's-BENCH, WESTMINSTER,

BEFORE THE

Hon. MR. JUSTICE BULLER,

AND A

SPECIAL JURY,

FOR A

CONSPIRACY

AGAINST THE

Right Hon. MARY ELEANOR BOWES,

COMMONLY CALLED

COUNTESS OF STRATHMORE.

TO WHICH ARE ADDED,

The Speeches of Mr ERSKINE, Mr CHAMBRE, and Mr FIELDING, in Mitigation of Punishment on Behalf of the Conspirators, and of Mr MINGAY, Mr LAW, and Mr. GARROW, in Support of the Prosecution, previous to the Judgment of the Court, on TUESDAY the 26th Day of June, which is also included

TAKEN IN SHORT HAND BY

E. HODGSON, SHORT HAND-WRITER to the SESSION at the OLD-BAILEY.

THE

TRIAL, &c.

COUNSEL FOR THE CROWN.

Mr. MINGAY, Mr. LAW, Mr. GARROW.

COUNSEL FOR THE DEFENDANTS.

Hon. T. ERSKINE, Mr. CHAMBRE, Mr. FIELDING.

Mr GARROW opened the Information.

Mr MINGAY opened the Cafe as follows:

MAY it pleafe your Lordfhip, and Gentlemen of the Jury, I am likewife of counfel in this cafe for the Crown, and it will be neceffary for me to ftate to you a tranfaction that I hope never, or any thing like it, exifted before in a chriftian country, it will therefore be neceffary for me, becaufe I dare fay that moft of you are not acquainted thoroughly with the nature of it, though you may have heard there has been fuch a thing depending, to ftate to you the fituation of the parties, the caufes that have produced, and the confequences that have followed, from the difputes that have arifen between this Lady and Andrew Robinfon Bowes   Gentlemen, before I do that, I will briefly ftate to you the charge againft thefe defendants——You have heard the pleadings opened by my learned friend, the fubftance of which is this, that Lady Strathmore having for fome time time lived apart from her hufband Mr. Bowes, a fuit was inftituted in the Confiftory Court of London, for a divorce, and that the defendants unlawfully confpiring together to hinder the further profecution of that fuit, and by means of force, violence, and imprifonment of her perfon, to compel her to drop it, that they did on the 10th of Novemoer make an affault upon her, feized and carried her away by force——that in order to compel her to drop this fuit, Mr. Bowes, affifted by a numerous gang, many of whom are now defendants, on the 10th of November laft, forcibly feized her, in the middle of the day, and in one of the moft public ftreets in London, dragged her fervants before a Juftice of the Peace, under a warrant, obtained by grofs perjury, and carried the unfortunate Lady, againft her will, near three hundred miles, through the heart of this king-dom; and before I ftate the circumftances of this cafe, I will inform you who all thefe defendants are——In the firft place, Andrew Robinfon Bowes is the hufband of Lady Strathmore, the fecond perfon is Edward Lucas, the conftable, the part he took in this bufinefs you will hear in the courfe of the detail, Francis Peacock is the agent of fome collieries in the north of England, and he was brought from the North to act a part in this fcene, Mark Provot is valet de chambre to Mr Bowes,

B   Cummings,

Cummins, who goes by the name of Chapman, together with Pigg, were dependents on Mr Bowes, Bickley is a Hackney coachman, Bourn is his steward, and Thomas Bowes is his attorney, living at Darlington, in the North These, Gentlemen, are the different actors in this infamous scene I call it infamous, and I will prove it so, for I am sure no man who hears me can, by any possibility of imagination, extend his mind so far in a course of iniquity, as to comprehend any thing like the present case. Gentlemen, this unfortunate lady, the object of their schemes, was the daughter of a Gentleman of an ancient family, who had a magnificent fortune in the North, and she first married Lord Strathmore, to whom she was not inferior, being one of the richest heiresses in the kingdom, after his death she unfortunately married Mr Andrew Robinson Bowes, and she continued to live with Mr. Bowes eight long and miserable years In 1785, after treatment that I should have thought no man could possibly have adopted against any woman, and that no woman, thank God, is bound to bear in this country from any man, she exhibited articles of the peace against him, he procured ample bail, the present Duke of Norfolk and my worthy friend Mr Lee—She instituted a suit in the Commons, for the purpose of obtaining a divorce against Mr Bowes, his securities were, that he should keep the peace for one year, in the course of that year every possible means were adopted to procrastinate that suit, and avoid its being determined, for, as Mr Bowes was conscious it could not be in his favor, therefore his sole object was delay, the suit came to a final hearing, and Mr Bowes then thought fit, for these gentlemen were his bail, and I will do him the justice to say, that as far as regarded the bail, he acted as a man of honor, I wish he had been uniform in that character towards his wife Gentlemen, in May 1786, the Judge of the Consistorial Court concluded the cause, and assigned the same for final sentence and hearing, he then appealed to the Arches Court of Canterbury, for the purpose of delay, on the last day of last Trinity Term the security expired, and he was no longer bound by the laws of his country so far as regarded his bail, as far as regarded them they were no longer under recognizances, and they were discharged. From that instant he meditated the plan which he afterwards executed, in the manner I shall state to you, he was determined to take the person of Lady Strathmore by force, to compel her by means as savage as they were uncommon and unheard of, to drop that suit in the Commons Gentlemen, upon his marriage with this Lady, in right of her Mr. Bowes came into the immediate possession of ten thousand pounds a year, and possessed that large income without making any settlement on her, therefore his object could not be her death, and I have often heard in this Court when these things have been discussed, what could Mr Bowes's possible motive be, if he did not want the death of Lady Strathmore? and I own it caught me, but if she was divorced in the Commons care would have been taken that part of that ten thousand a year should go to the Lady, his object was that she should drop that suit, and continue to live with him as his wife, and he have the power and controul over it all Gentlemen, it was impossible for any man to execute so grand a scene as this without some men of his own description, as soon therefore as he had done his business here with respect to his bail and their recognizances, as soon as he had settled some causes in Durham, or thereabouts, he comes to town, and brings very respectable companions along with him, he brings Mr. Peacock, an agent in the North, he brings Provot, his valet de chambre, he brings with him Cummins, otherwise Chapman, and Pigg, who were people that were accustomed to deeds of darkness by living in a mine. In his way to town it occurred to Mr. Bowes, that he had travelled that road too often, and that bringing these people from the North would naturally excite suspicion and curiosity, he therefore came a bye road, puts on a large bush wig with a long tail, and passed for Colonel Medison, he came to Stone in Staffordshire, and there he hired a poor lad, who will be called to you, his name is Peter Orme, this lad came to town hired by Colonel Medison and Mr Peacock, who took upon himself the name of Johnson, this boy by appointment came to the Swan with Two Necks in Lad-Lane. It is necessary to be thus particular, because I must state these things to you, and you will see the part that Bourn and Thomas Bowes acted, in order to satisfy your minds that they conspired and acted, though not in London, to bring this scheme into execution, for God forbid, that in a case like this, any man that can be reached by the laws of his country should escape. When this lad got to town, they brought him to their house in Norfolk-street in the Strand, which was hired for the purpose—says Bowes my horses are not yet come to town, and till they come from grass, I shall not want your assistance, but by no means stir out of the house. While they were in

the

the house in Norfolk-street, these persons went out continually, always disguised and always armed, to observe Lady Strathmore's motions, her Ladyship was then living at a house in Bloomsbury-Square, and their sole object was to seize her person Gentlemen, Mr Bowes in the course of these proceedings, at different times put on different disguises, for the purpose that while he was watching around the house, because she was very much on her guard, for the purpose of eluding her observations, he appeared as Colonel Medison, he took upon himself the disguise of an old man in a large wig, had spectacles, as a justice of the peace, and at last h t on the disguise of a sailor! How the Devil (for nobody but the Devil could devise such schemes as these) I say how the Devil could put it in his head to think of a sailor he must explain to you, a most unnatural disguise for such a project, and more peculiarly so as the object of his persecution was a woman—creatures of all others most beloved by British tars They were once in a coach with the blinds up, and disguised, somebody gave Lady Strathmore intelligence, and she was prevented from going abroad that day, and of course she was naturally suspicious that some mischief was intended her, and you will now see what an artful scheme was adopted by Mr Bowes. With respect to Mr Thomas Bowes and Mr Bourn, you will find circumstances are necessary to be attended to, for undoubtedly their cases are different from the rest, for they, though not busy actors, were most undoubtedly behind the curtain Lady Strathmore upon these suspicions, through her attorney, applied to me (having had the honour of being long concerned for her as one of her council) and I own it did not occur to me that she could apply to the Court, because no violence had been offered to her person, and who those people were that were shut up in a coach she could not tell, she was very unwilling to stir abroad but for the necessity of her health —Mr. Bowes, conscious this would be the case, had another scene to act, he therefore leaves Chapman, Peacock, and Pigg, at their head quarters in Norfolk-street, he goes in the night directly into the North, immediately after this, when he found that he was suspected, he takes Prevot, and Bickley, this hackney coachman, and Orme, with him, when he got to the Cock at Eaton, he left Bickley and Orme behind him, and Prevot and he went directly for the North, his object was to shew himself publicly in the North, and that he might be seen at Barnard-Castle on such a day They arrived at Lady Strathmore's house, which is his in her right, he goes publicly the next morning to Barnard-Castle Market, this was not enough, he had a further scheme, he not only wished to satisfy the people that were in London that he was in the North, and doing no mischief, but he could not stay in the North, because if he had, the mischief could not be carried on in the South, so he sees a Mr Colpits, says he, this is the time, he got off his horse, and lays himself down on the road, carefully enough, I dare say! Bourn rides up to Mr Colpits, Good God! here is a dreadful accident! Mr Bowes has broke his leg, and every thing but his neck! Bourn rides away for a surgeon—he fetches a surgeon, and he will tell you that he pretended to bleed him—says he, he has broke three of his ribs, he has dislocated his shoulder, and fractured his skull, Lord have mercy upon me! He was carried to Streatlam Castle, the night coming on favoured him very much, every body enquired after his health, and my learned friend Mr Lee, who is his neighbour, from that goodness of heart which actuates him in every thing, sent to enquire also, nobody could see him, he was too bad to be seen—nobody was to see him except Thomas Bowes, his attorney; and I will prove to you, that while this farce was acting, Thomas Bowes was present in the Castle, and the only person, except Bourn the Steward, that was admitted into it, it was put into all the papers—and Gentlemen, Mr Hobson, is one of the most astonishing surgeons in the world, for on the 28th of October, through the assistance of Mr. Hobson, Mr. Bowes was back again at the Cock at Eaton, the Castle was shut up, inquiries were carried on—he is a little better, but not well enough to be seen, and all this that he might come back to London, and make this unmanly attack upon Lady Strathmore's person. Gentlemen, they all came back to Norfolk-street, and there they met, and then determined to carry this plan into execution on the 30th or 31st of October, two days after they came back from the North. It was necessary for them, if they possibly could, to get into some situation by way of residence, where they might observe the situation of Lady Strathmore, and they went to the back of Bloomsbury-Square all in disguise, and they applied to a man of the name of Crooke, they asked him to let them a lodging—Crooke said, upon my soul I took them for a gang of thieves, and I would have nothing to do with them, they said

they

they had come five or six hundred miles in pursuit of robbers, Crooke had no objection to calling on them with information, and they told him to enquire for the Justice, and when he went, there was Mr Bowes sitting in a great arm chair, Col. Medison in a great wig and long tail, he was the justice, and Pigg, whose history you have heard, was with him. Gentlemen, I understand this man was permitted to be sworn to secrecy, for Mr Bowes, I understand, travels about with a book with him, and swears the people to secrecy, they offered this man money, they shook a purse at him, he looked at it, he took it for Pandora's box, he thought there was something at the bottom that would bite him, when they found they could get no ends answered by him, they asked him—can you recommend us a constable? so he turned it over in his mind—says he, I know one Lucas, and Gentlemen, if there can be in things that are extremely infamous, any thing that is more infamous than the rest, I think it is the part of Lucas, he was introduced by Crooke to Mr. Bowes, he had a very great reward promised him, and he was very much tempted by it, he was to do this as being a peace officer—he was to get acquainted with Lady Strathmore, warn her of her danger, and promise and offer her his services, his reward was this, he was to have some houses that belonged to Lady Strathmore at a pepper corn rent, till Mr Bowes got him a place in the Custom-House of equal value, and I will prove to you, that Mr Bowes went to the tenants, and told them Lucas was their landlord, and he had afterwards the impudence to demand the rent. On the first of November Lucas went to Lady Strathmore, and pretended he had seen some lurking fellows, says he, "My Lady, they are very ill-looking fellows, they look as if they deserve to be hanged," this far, Gentlemen, he spoke true, "they must have something very infamous in view," so far he spoke true, and he imposed upon her so far as actually to put herself under his protection, and to pay him from time to time to go backwards and forwards and give her notice. Now it is necessary to state to you the names of the servants that were in the house of Lady Strathmore, because you will find bye-and-bye, that this scheme was put into execution by that which is terrible to state in a Court of Justice, for by perjury this deed was carried into execution. Gentlemen, Mrs Morgan was upper servant and companion to Lady Strathmore, Robert Crundel was her footman, Daniel Lee was her coachman—Bowes did not know his name, but he gave him a name—on the eighth of November, Chapman, one of the defendants, assuming the name of Cummins, went to the office of Mr Walker, who, I understand, is a respectable magistrate in this county, and he there made oath that he went in danger of his life from Mary Morgan, Crundel and Jones—the name of the man was Lee, but however he was taken under the name of Jones, as coachman, upon which the warrant was granted, it was given to Lucas of course, you know Lucas could not himself take Mrs Morgan, the coachman and footman of Lady Strathmore, that would have been out of his power, he therefore employed one Broad, and agreed to pay him a guinea a day for his trouble, he likewise employed Saunders and Mecham, on the same day, the 10th of November, Lucas went to Lady Strathmore's to know if she was going out, he said he would protect her and defend her, she paid him for his former attendances, and said, I do not mean to trouble you to-day, Captain Farrer is so obliging to take an airing with me to day, he is sufficient to protect me. Lucas goes and tells them of their intended airing, the consequence was, Lady Strathmore went out, Lucas watched the carriage with the rest of these people, the coach drove to the house of Mr. Foster in Oxford-street, Lady Strathmore and Mrs Morgan got out, and the coachman and footman were immediately seized and taken before a magistrate, Lady Strathmore was left in the house with Mrs Morgan, they ran up stairs necessarily, apprehending danger, their friend Lucas came up to the door, and he tapped, "Who's there?" "Your friend Lucas," says he, "Oh, Lucas, open the door," the very instant they opened the door, he said "he had a warrant against her, and she must be carried to Lord Mansfield's, that it was as much as his life was worth not to execute it, and, as for you, Mrs Morgan," says he, "I advise you to go away, for there are more warrants against you." She went away, Lady Strathmore was left with Captain Farrer—says he to Captain Farrer, "I charge you to aid and assist me in the King's name, we are only going to Caen Wood." One of these men was put on the coach box, another behind, Lucas got into the coach with Lady Strathmore and Captain Farrer, when they got to Highgate, they were met by Mr. Bowes and Provot. Lady Strathmore cried out, she broke the window, she used every possible means to escape from the hands of these ruffians, but in vain, she was forced on

the

the north road, she was forced on from stage to stage, in a manner it will be unnecessary for me to state to you, I shall prove it by witnesses. Mr Bowes joined them at Highgate, they pretended to drive on to Lord Mansfield's, instead of which they went on towards Barnet, and when they got near Barnet Captain Farrer was desired, with a blunderbuss at his head, to get out, he was obliged to walk back again, and they drove on, all these people were armed, and it is impossible for any man if he was in such a situation to feel to that extent that a poor and miserable timid woman would do, in the hands of such people. Gentlemen, as he went along at different places, when people necessarily enquired—what is all this? for she screamed most violently. Mr Bowes made use of the old scheme, said she was mad, a poor unhappy woman, so the people let her pass. Gentlemen, on the 11th of November, at twelve at night, they arrived at Streatlam Castle, there they were met by Mr Bourn, the Steward, and Mary Gowland, an excellent companion for the wife of Mr Bowes, for she, I believe, has been just brought to bed of a bastard child by the husband—husband, did I say?—a satyr—He took her into the dining room, he put a pistol to her head—he had before endeavoured to prevail upon her to sign a paper, which she persisted to refuse, she declared she never would sign any thing, and you will find that at Stilton he attempted it on the road, when he got her into the room by herself, he used all possible means, he held a pistol to her head, she said she would not—she refused it a second time, he desired her to say her prayers, for he would put her to death—she said she would not sign any paper, she said her prayers, and she said to Mr Bowes, fire!—with a courage that to me is astonishing! upon which he—even he exclaimed, by God you are an astonishing woman! the answer to that would have been obvious, but I dare say she dared not to make it. Gentlemen, thus he dragged her about, Mr Chapman and Mr Pigg carried her to bed, they were two Abigails she had not been used to before, and I will prove to you, that he actually pleaded, that during this very infamous misconduct of his, that she had cohabited with him on mountains and in snow, that she had cohabited with him from *the 12th to the 20th of November, in a state of mutual forgiveness. Gentleman,* if that had been true, the suit in the Commons would have cut a very indifferent figure on the behalf of Lady Strathmore, and I dare say that some attempts will be given in evidence to induce you to believe it, but, Gentlemen, if Mr Bowes did with violence get between the sheets in the presence of these fellows, it will be for you to say whether there is a colour to assert—whether in such a situation, she could have consented to the addresses of such a man?—She refused him, she told him he should not, and said to him, " If you do not desist—for I know your purpose well—I know your object, if you cannot compel me by force to give up my suit, you may notwithstanding, compel me to that which is called cohabitation, and if you do, I will indict you for a rape," and there are cases where a husband is liable to be tried for a rape even on his own wife, as much as if he had forced any other woman, this frightened him a little, for his own good was very much at heart, he did not wish to get into the scrape of being hanged, upon this he had to debate a little in his own mind how he should pursue this Lady, if I can neither by force compel her to cohabit with me, or drop her suit, what course can I take? Why I will get her abroad, I will send her to Ireland, that was the only chance he had, for the alarm was given here, expresses were sent, and pains taken, that was the object of Mr Farrer,—As soon as he could, he applied to this Court, and she was rescued afterwards in a manner marvellous; most undoubtedly his scheme was to have carried her abroad, if he could have effected that purpose, he took her, he left some of his confederates in the Castle, and they were to practise this scheme, and it was to be given out that Lady Strathmore was in the Castle, that they might not attempt to rescue her. In the dead of the night, therefore, Mr Bowes set out, he took her, made her get up, hurry on a few of her cloaths, put on an old bonnet belonging to some servant, and Providence—certainly it is Providence which watches over us all that orders it so, that when ever you see men in these situations, circumstances seemingly small, tend to confirm their guilt, for a great coat was put on this Lady, which turns out to be the great coat of Thomas Bowes, the attorney, I cannot prove that he was there by positive evidence, but I will lay such circumstances before you, that shall leave no doubt in your minds that he was there, in this great coat this Lady was wrapped up, in the North of England. at that time of the year, she was very near frozen to death, she was mounted on a horse behind somebody, in the dead of night, she cannot tell who, she rather thinks

C

't was Mr Bowes, prefently Bourn, the Steward, joins them, and they went to the houfe of the father of this Mary Gowland, a harlot who lived with Mr. Bowes, fhe was treated there moft brutally. On the 13th of November, he faid it was in vain to refift, I have you in my power, unlefs you confent I will fend for a mad doctor, I will put you on a ftrait waiftcoat, but, Gentlemen, any punifhment upon earth, a ftrait waiftcoat, Bedlam, the moft dreadful ftate of a human being, appeared to her to be abfolute Paradife, in comparifon to living with Mr. Bowes. Gentlemen, he afterwards took her and dragged her over fuch a country, covered with fnow and fleet continually, at laft he found he had dragged her too far for his purpofe, for fhe was very near dead, fhe was very near frozen, he took fome gin, and fhe inftructs me to fay, that it is a liquor fhe had never tafted before, but in that ftate of mifery, cold, perifhing, fhe drank fome of it, it warmed her, it kept her alive, he took her over mountains and precipices to Appleby, and had her put to the fire and fhe recovered a little, there he took the name of Doctor Hopper, a mad doctor, with a lady under his care, the parties were then got to Appleby, and before I ftate to you the further progrefs of this bufinefs, it will be neceffary for me to relate to you the part that Thomas Bowes, the attorney took: about this time a letter had been fent to Mr. Thomas Bowes, and from the receipt of that letter Mr. Ripon, who was his clerk, and whom I fhall call as a witnefs, difcovered a vaft profundity of thought about him, a great deal of thinking, fomething like what Salluft fpeaks of, who, I dare fay, you have all read, walking very quick, and then very flow, marks of a perturbed mind, and he forbid his clerk from going into his office, Ripon thought that very extraordinary,—Gentlemen, that is but a circumftance, but it will be for you to fay, whether you do not believe he was at the bottom of this iniquitous tranfaction. I have related to you the circumftance of the great coat, and another thing I fhall be able to prove to you, that on the very day Mr. Bowes left Streatlam Caftle, he was in the Caftle, in clofe converfation with Thomas Bowes, I cannot prove what they faid, but a very little time before Mr Bowes went from the caftle, he went into the chamber of Peter Orme, and cried out "Thomas, Thomas" Peter Orme faid, "My name is not Thomas" Peter Orme got up, and Thomas Bowes went into another room, and was in clofe converfation with Chapman and Pigg. Gentlemen I ftate thefe circumftances to you, that you may be able to apply them when you hear them given in evidence, to fatisfy your minds that he was a party in thefe tranfactions. The next day Bourn, the fteward, who had gone off with Lady Strathmore and Mr Bowes, came back to the Caftle, Thomas Bowes and Orme continued in the Caftle, the only two people that were left there, the Caftle was fhut up, and no creature was permitted to enter it—but there was an animal that is very apt to make his way every where, and that was a tipftaff of this Court, he afterwards fwore that he had ferved Mr. Bowes—that was not true at that time—but this Thomas Bowes had made himfelf fo very like Mr Bowes, that Ridgeway miftook, and it was very natural he fhould, upon this Ridgeway cries out, "he wants Mr Bowes, he is come with a Habeas Corpus, defires to know if Mr. Andrew Robinfon Bowes is in the houfe," to which Mr Thomas Bowes fays, "Mr Bowes is not to be feen or fpoke to." Gentlemen, that is not the conduct of an innocent man, but, in the courfe of the argument, one of my learned friends fuggefted, "Oh, Mr. Bowes was afraid of being arrefted for ten pounds," a contemptible idea! I will prove to you that Peter Orme found the information of the Court, and the Rules and Habeas Corpus, pufhed under the door, and gave them to Thomas Bowes, the attorney, why, Gentlemen, do you think he did not know an Habeas Corpus, but he burnt his fingers with them, and returned them to Peter Orme—fays he, "take them, and put them where you found them." In the courfe of a little while, Lady Strathmore's friends got about, every body was in arms, every body was about the Caftle, and Mr. Bowes had no curiofity about him, not the leaft, and you are to fuppofe that Thomas Bowes, the attorney, was innocently locked up in this Caftle, with Pigg and Chapman, Bourn and Orme, that Mr Bowes was gone without his knowledge, and a mob of many hundreds, nay thoufands of colliers, and people who had remembered the father and family and worked there, were affembled thereabouts, were affembled for the purpofe of dragging her from the hands of ruffians, yet he never afks a fingle queftion, he keeps the Caftle locked up, he himfelf is the Conftable of the Tower, till Mr. Farrer came, who is a native of

the

the place, he admitted him to come in on his parole, for the purpose of conversing with him, and no one else.—Is this the conduct of an innocent man?—Is this the conduct of a person who supposed that every thing was fair and honest that was transacted in that Castle? Gentlemen, I find too that Mr Bourn, the Steward, had not the curiosity to enquire neither. Gentlemen, there they continued till the 16th of November—was not he wanted at Darlington about his business? No, he had shut up his office, and forbid his clerk to enter; he certainly could have no great business transacting there, or at least that sort of business that would not bear the light.—Gentlemen, if Thomas Bowes should escape by the assistance of my learned friend Mr Erskine, and his assistance will be as great as any man's in our profession, I say, if he should escape by his assistance, it will be a very wonderful thing under these circumstances, and I trust it is what cannot possibly happen. Gentlemen, after Mr Farrer had got admittance into the Castle, and then questioned those gentlemen where is Lady Strathmore? both Bourn and Thomas Bowes positively refused to answer any questions at all, you will wonder why I take all this pains, but I know the arguments that will be made use of, I do not know that I shall have an opportunity of addressing you again—I know the impression that will most probably be made by the eloquence of my learned friend. If Mr Thomas Bowes had been an honorable and an honest man, why refuse to answer fair questions put to him about Lady Strathmore? No—they both of them refuse to answer interrogatories; that is just the thing we may expect from an attorney, so Bowes the Attorney said to Mr. Farrer, upon his oath, Gentlemen—I shall support this by evidence most clearly —they are not arguments founded upon imagination. I think it impossible for any man with any hopes of success, to lift up his voice for the defendants, against such evidence.—We must now return to Appleby—as soon as they left that place she was taken on the road that leads to a place called Penrith, (and a few miles distant from the former place) he was informed that he was pursued, he immediately stopped and forced her out of the chaise, he put her behind Chapman on the horse's bare back, and hid her in a cow-house, they bundled her in as a bale of goods—there is no talking of this with patience as a man. He then took her and dragged her over the top of some mountains that were covered with snow, till she was very near perished; at last they arrived at Darlington, he found they were pursued, and found it would be in vain to continue his route, he came to Darlington about four in the morning on the 19th of November, and they went to Thomas Bowes's house, she was kept a considerable time in the dark, and this honest man—this husband! has indicted this Lady for perjury, for she swore she was kept in a dark room, and she was put into a pig stye, and put into a stable—the fact was, she was kept in a dark passage, frozen almost to death, and perishing, her mind distracted, she was taken into a stack yard where pigs were kept—not in a pig stye, but I shall call the farmer to prove there was a large herd of swine grunting round her—she was kept with hogs, pigs, and sows round about her—what could she have thought? I will, for a moment, suppose her the most abandoned prostitute that the earth ever produced, but for a man to treat a woman thus, what must be every honest man's sensations? With respect to her being put into a stable, she was put into a shed where there were horses, and yet these trifling trumpery things are made the subject of the indictment for perjury! and she is to stand here to take the trial of her country, after you have disposed of this case. Gentlemen, I ask whether she is not the most persecuted woman that ever was? He took her from Thomas Bowes's house to Durham and Newcastle, and at that place he turned postillion in the way to Harlow-Hill in Northumberland, he there, at three in the morning, desired the boys to drive him across the country to Morpeth, in the same county, the boys started at it—Good God, Sir, it is as much as our lives are worth—we cannot go—we will not go, and they absolutely refused to go, on account of the inclement season—but less inclement than her persecutor. This miserable woman, that had been sitting in the chaise in the stack yard for upwards of four long and tedious hours, almost frozen to death, worn out with famine and fatigue, while he and his companions, except one that was set to watch her, were gone into the hovel for shelter. On the boys refusal, it was necessary for Bowes to take some step himself, he therefore determines to return to Newcastle, and from thence went through Durham towards Darlington, but being closely pursued, they were refused horses; nobody would venture abroad, as King Lear said, " In such a night as this to turn me out!" Good God, Gentlemen! Such monsters are too shocking to think of. In the stage between Durham and Darlington, they were refused horses, Bourn the steward came

up

up and gave the alarm, and told him they were purfued, and I fhall prove the fteward faid the country people were up, and that Lady Strathmore will be refcued. She was then taken by Bowes, and he mounted her behind him, till at laft, with the activity of the purfuers, and by that vigilant hand of Providence, that protects the innocent almoft always, at laft Mr Bowes was taken with great hazard. He prefented a piftol, or fome other weapon, and threatened to put a countryman who attacked him to death, but this deterred him not, he was armed with that fearful weapon honeftly—Oh! they are dreadful odds!—a ftraw in the hands of an honeft countryman is equal to all the fire arms in the hands of Bowes, and Lady Strathmore was refcued. when fhe arrived at Mr Farrer's he will tell you her fituation, for I fhould excite thofe feelings that muft divert your attention, and you would give way to that fort of fenfibility natural from the defcription—but you fhall hear it from the witnefs, and from thence you will collect the cafe, from feeing her when fhe was brought back, from hearing every ftage fhe went through, and then you will judge whether he was from the 12th of November to the 20th living with her in a ftate of *mutual cohabitation and forgivenefs* !

Gentlemen, Lady Strathmore now brings this Cafe before my Lord and you, and I underftand there is another indictment for perjury found againft her at the Old Bailey on Saturday laft, Mr Bowes applied for a Warrant, whether that indictment was well or ill founded I cannot tell—I only obferve that men who are capable of aiding fuch a man as this, are capable of fwearing any thing, and by that, as well as all the reft, you fee the perfecutions, the fcandalous perfecutions of this unhappy woman from her hufband—Gentlemen, I am afraid I have fatigued you, and that you will tire before the Caufe is over, I will not call to you more witneffes than is neceffary—I believe I have here in this place people of all defcriptions who have feen this transaction, who are come here as willing witneffes to ftate what they have obferved in the cafe, but for the purpofe of conviction it will not be neceffary to call them all, probably I fhall be able to fatisfy your minds by calling to you a very inconfiderable number. Lady Strathmore has been thus compelled to bring them before my Lord and you, and I truft you will afford her protection and affiftance, that you will do it by your verdict of conviction, and when that is the cafe I do not doubt but the Court hereafter will fee thefe defendants in their proper colours, and will treat them as they deferve, and will teach them that fuch glaring and audacious violation of the laws cannot in this country efcape with impunity.

Dr MARKHAM *fworn, to prove the Marriage.*

Mr LAW Q. Did you examine that Paper with the Regifter ?
A I did with the Parifh Regifter of St. James's, Weftminfter.
Q. Is it a true Copy ?
A It is (the Paper contained a copy of the entry of the marriage between Andrew Robinfon Bowes, Efq and Lady Strathmore in the year 1777)

MARK HOLMAN, *fworn, (produces the Affignation Book of the Confiftory Court of the Bifhop of London)*

Mr. GARROW Q. What are you?
A The Regifter of that Court
Q. Is there any caufe now depending between Lady Strathmore and Mr Bowes ?
A There is, that is the original Citation taken out by her Ladyfhip againft him the 28th of February 1785, to anfwer to the Right Hon. Mary Eleanor Bowes, commonly called Countefs of Strathmore, by reafon of adultery and cruel treatment
(*Mr Stephens referred to his Affignation Book of the Arches Court of Canterbury*)
Q. Is any caufe now depending, or was it depending on the 10th of November laft ?
A On the 10th of November 1786, it was waiting for the appeal to the Court of Arches, Mr. Bowes gave in an allegation of mutual forgivenefs, that they had cohabited together fince the 10th of November, and it is figned by him.
Mr ERSKINE. Q. Have you all the proceedings of that Court here ?
A. Up to that period, the Allegation is dated the 30th of November 1786.
Q. He did not fwear to the truth of it ?
A. No, he did not

PETER ORME *sworn.*

Mr Garrow. Q. What are you?
A. A post-boy.
Q. Where did you live in October last?
A. At Stone, in Staffordshire.
Q. Do you know Mr. Bowes, the defendant?
A. Yes.
Q. Relate where you first saw him.
A. At Stone, in Staffordshire, in October last—On the 14th of October last, Mr Bowes came to Stone, under the name of Colonel Medison there were with him, Francis Peacock, who went by the name of Mr Johnson—there was one Charles Chapman and William Pigg, and another person whose name I do not recollect.
Q. State what passed between you, and Mr Bowes, and these persons at Stone?
A. There were no words passed with us at Stone, I drove him a stage, and he asked me whether I wanted a place, the man did belonging to him—I told him yes; I should have no objection to going along with a gentleman, and he hired me to be a groom to him—he sent for me into the room, and hired me to be his groom, he told me he would give me twenty guineas a-year, and a guinea in hand, and accordingly he gave me a guinea in hand, and gave me directions to come to the Swan with two Necks in Lad-lane—I came, and saw Mr Bowes there, on the Sunday; I came to London on the 15th, that was on Sunday—I saw Mr Bowes the same day that I came to London—He met me at the Swan with two Necks, there were Peacock and Prevot—they took me to the Grand Hotel in Covent-Garden—I staid there all night, the next morning I went to Norfolk-street, Strand, to No 18.
Q. How long did you continue to live with Mr Bowes, at Norfolk-street?
A. About a month.
Q. How was you employed?
A. To keep in the house—I staid at home—I went out with him sometimes.
Q. Did Mr Bowes go out frequently?
A. Yes, they went out in Hackney coaches, they passed by the name of Colonel Medison—Peacock went by the name of Johnson—Mr Bowes was sometimes disguised in a sailor's dress, and sometimes he had a wig, a large wig, over his hair
Q. Had they any arms with them when they went out?
A. Yes.
Q. What sort of arms?
A. Generally a brace of horse pistols, and a small-sword, Mr Bowes had.
Q. They used frequently to go out in Hackney coaches?
A. Frequently, with the blinds half-way up—they used to go to Hyde-park-corner, the King's-road and Chelsea—they looked about to see if they could see the persons they wanted—they informed me it was somebody that had robbed Colonel Medison of his plate, and they were in pursuit of these persons.
Q. Did your coach wait at the places?
A. Yes, sometimes three, four, or five hours.
Q. At that time who has been in the coach?
A. Sometimes Mr Bowes in one coach, and some of the men in another—Chapman, and Peacock and Prevot
Q. How often were these sort of things repeated?
A. They used sometimes to go out every day.
Q. What business did you do then?
A. I went out with them sometimes
Q. Do you remember being with them on the 23d of October, in Bloomsbury-square?
A. Yes, Sir, it was on a Sunday, but I cannot tell the date—there was Colonel Medison and Mr Johnson, and a little man along with them, I shall know him when I see him, it was not Lucas.
Q. What did you do that day?

D

A. I drove

A. I drove them—I cannot tell where I drove them to, but I follo̫ed a carriage by Mr Bowes's direction—I have since learned whose carriage it was—he ordered me to follow it where it went to

Q Whose carriage was it?

A Lady Strathmore's, I understand now?

Q Did you go with Mr Bowes to Eaton at any time?

A Yes—I cannot tell the day of the month, it was the evening of the same month that I followed Lady Strathmore's carriage, we left town about ten in the evening—there was Mr Bowes, Prevot, me, and John Bickley, Bickley and me went on saddle horses, Mr Bowes and Prevot went in a post-chaise—we got to the Cock, at Eaton, between six and seven in the the morning—me and Bickley were left there, Mr Bowes and Prevot went forward to the North road—we continued there till the Saturday following, then I saw Mr. Bowes, he came between six and seven in the morning, Prevot came back with him, then we came to town, altogether, the same way we had gone down

Q Did you return to Norfolk-street?

A Yes.

Q Did you continue living there in the same manner you had done before?

A. Yes.

Q How was Bowes dressed then—He was the Colonel still?

A Yes, Sir—He had a drab great coat on, and a pair of trowsers.

Q. Had Mr Bowes his own hair?

A. Yes—then he had a wig on—I returned to London, and continued in the same way I had before

Q State all the proceedings of the day Lady Strathmore was taken.

A. It was the 10th of November, I believe it was in the morning, he ordered me to get a pair of horses from Water-Lane, I had a pair of bay horses, he ordered me to take them up to St Giles's and get a chaise, and wait at the Turnpike at Tottenham-Court, on the road to Barnet, till he came up, I waited there about four hours, I got there between ten and eleven in the forenoon, I saw Mr Bowes between two and three in the evening, there came a large carriage full speed, and a hackney coach after it Mr Bowes beckoned me with his finger to follow him with the post-chaise, Mr. Bowes was in the hackney-coach, the other coach I have since learned was Lady Strathmore's, I followed and drove till I came half way up Highgate-Hill, then Mr Bowes got out and got into the post-chaise, there was Prevot and Johnson, that is Peacock, and Chapman, and William Pigg was behind my Lady's carriage.

Q In what manner was Mr. Bowes dressed at that time?

A He was in black cloaths.

Q Any disguise?

A No, but when he passed me at the Turnpike he had his great wig and his drab coloured coat on, he pulled that off, and came into my post-chaise, then I went up Highgate-Hill, and stopped at Highgate, at Highgate my Lady got out into a room there, and threw up the sash, and cried out murder, several times, I cannot say whether it was Mr Bowes or Lucas that pulled my Lady away, I had seen Lucas before in Norfolk-street, he had been several times with the Colonel, towards the latter part of it Lucas was very frequently there. At Highgate after her Ladyship came out of the house, they took and put her into her own coach, Colonel Medison got in with her and Lucas, there was a Gentleman with her Ladyship, he got in and went a little way with her from Highgate, I drove the post-chaise, in that there were Peacock and Prevot, and that little man whose name I do not know, we drove to the Red Lion at Barnet.

Q. Were any of these persons armed at this time?

A. Yes, they had arms in the chaise with them.

Q In both the carriages?

A Yes, I believe Lucas had a pistol of Mr. Farrer's, they had all of them arms; we went at last as far as Streatlam Castle.

Q How long was you performing that journey?

A. I cannot tell how many hours, my Lady cried out murder, she refused to get out—she cried out murder—Mr Bowes and Chapman put her in by force, she seemed much changed in colour, and to go much against her will.

Q She seemed much agitated?

A. Yes.

Q During

Q. During this time, you say, you took Mr. Bowes to be Colonel Medison?

A. Yes, I first discovered him at Barnet, a gentleman came up on horseback, and asked if that was not Mr Bowes and Lady Strathmore.

Q. What day did you get to Streatlam Castle?

A. It was on the Saturday night, I continued there and saw Mr. Bowes on the Sunday morning walking about in the passage at Streatlam Castle, I continued there four days, I do not remember the time when Lady Strathmore was carried away from there—I was in bed, I left London the 10th of November, and got there on Saturday night—I do not remember her being taken out of the Castle.

Q. Do you remember Mr Thomas Bowes?

A. Yes, I know him now.

Q. Do you remember seeing him at Streatlam Castle?

A. Yes.

Q. Was he there while Lady Strathmore was there?

A. I cannot tell, I saw him there on the Monday morning when I came down stairs from the room, he came to me in the middle of the night, he came into the room—I was in bed, and he called out, Thomas, Thomas, several times, Thomas—I told him my name was not Thomas, so he went into the next room, to the men in the next room, where Chapman and Pigg lay, and a man of the name of Joseph, he continued there some time with them—they had some conversation which I could not hear.

Q. When did you come away from Streatlam Castle?

A. On Thursday

Q. Had you any conversation with Mr Bowes on the Monday morning after he came into your room?

A. Yes, he came into the room and he asked me to sit down, so I did, I asked him whether the French servant was got up, he said he was not, I began to be uneasy to think that I could not see any body, there was nobody in the place.

Q. Had you any idea of the plan, or did you mean to assist?

A. Not the least in the world.

Q. Have you seen Lucas lately?

A. Yes, I saw him the night before last.

Q. Where?

A. At Mr. Conner's, the Mitre at Barnet, I live at present with Mr. Broughton, at the Red Lion—Conner sent for me the night before last.

Q. Had you any conversation with Conner or Lucas, in the presence of Lucas?

A. This was before I saw Lucas

Q. What passed between you and Lucas the night before last?

A. Mr Conner said to Lucas, this is the young man that I believe was servant to Mr. Bowes—says he, I do not recollect him—says I, if you do not, I recollect you when you got out of the carriage at Stilton,—so he said, indeed young man I do not recollect you, so he turned up his eyes at me, so, with his spectacles, and he called for some brandy and water, and asked me if I should like to see Mr Bowes, he was sure Mr Bowes would satisfy me for my trouble, and the wages he owed me, and every thing, if I would go with them, I told them that I must be here, and they said I had no occasion to do that, if I had a mind to be out of the way—Conner said that in the hearing of Lucas.

Q. Did they say any thing more about it?

A. No, Sir, I live at present with Mr. Broughton—they asked me how long I had lived with him, I told them a little before Christmas.

Q. Did Lady Strathmore appear to be going with her will?

A. No, it was against her will, and she cried out murder in several places, and particularly at Stilton—she was forced into the carriage against her will by Mr. Bowes and another.

Q. Do you remember seeing any paper at Streatlam Castle while you was there?

A. Yes, I found a paper that had been put under the door, I took it to Mr Thomas Bowes, and he ordered me to put it where I had it.

Q. What did he say?

A. He said, you go and take that where you had it, for I have nothing to do with it.

Q. That was before the persons came in to search the house?

A. It might be about three or four hours the same day, it was a paper with some writing upon it, I found it about nine.

Q. Was

Q. Was you there when Mr. Farrer came in ?

A Yes, I was.

Q Did you hear any body from without demanding entrance ?

A Yes, I heard fomebody demanding the body of Lady Strathmore ?

Q Was that demand made before you found thefe papers ?

A It was after—it was made fevera' times—I know Mr Bourn, I faw him at the Steward's room in Streatlam Caftle, he continued there till Mr Farrer got in—I heard no particular converfation

Mr. ERSKINE Q. You was hired, you fay, by Mr. Bowes in the character of Colonel Medifon ?

A. Yes.

Q You came to town and acted perfectly innocent, as far as your own notions went ?

A. Yes

Q You did not know who Lady Strathmore was ?

A. I did not.

Q You did not know Lady Strathmore was the wife of Mr. Bowes ?

A No, that was not communicated to me.

Q Nothing of that fort ?

A. No, Sir, it was not

Q When you came to Streatlam, of courfe you knew who Mr. Bowes was ?

A. Yes ?

Q When did you firft know his name was Bowes ?

A. At Barnet.

Q When did you firft know fhe was his wife ?

A At Barnet

Q Then you knew that Mr Bowes was carrying his wife in this manner ?

A. Yes

Q And you made no complaint to the inn-keeper for the purpofe of refcuing this Lady ?

A. No, I did not.

Q When you came to the Caftle, Lady Strathmore and Mr Bowes went into the apartments in the Caftle ?

A Yes.

Q I fuppofe you did not go with them ?

A No

Q Did you ever fee them at Streatlam Caftle ?

A. I faw Mr. Bowes on the Sunday morning, but I never faw her Ladyfhip afterwards ?

Q Then how fhe was treated there you cannot tell ?

A. I cannot tell.

Q Mr. Thomas Bowes came into your room ?

A Yes, between twelve and one

Q. And called out Thomas ?

A. Yes.

Q. And then went into the room with the other two people ?

A Yes.

Q. You had no converfation at all with Mr. Bowes ?

A Yes, on the Monday morning.

Q How did Lady Strathmore get out of her carriage ?

A. She walked out, and as fhe was going into the Caftle fhe cried out fome time.

Q. You did not fee Mr Bowes till he came into your room ?

A Not Mr. Thomas Bowes, I did not.

Q You never faw Lady Strathmore again ?

A I did not fee them together.

JURY Q During the time you was in the fervice, did you wear the regular livery of Mr Bowes ?

A No, I wore my own cloaths.

Q What was the diftance that you drove from three to the next night ?

A I cannot tell, about 240 miles.

Mr.

Mr ERSKINE.   Q There was a great mob for feveral days?

A. Yes.

Q Fires lighted?

A Yes.

Q And threats to the people in the Caftle?

A, No, no threats—There might be an hundred people—The doors were fhut and faftened within fide

Q Did not a vaft number of people call out that they would have Lady Strathmore, dead or alive?

A They did.

Q Did you hear them fay what they would do to Bourn?

A No.

Mr GARROW   Q Were the doors faftened before the mob affembled?

A. Yes

Q As foon as you got in?

A As foon as I faw them come about.

Q What ftate were the window-fhutters in?

A. They were all faftened with iron bars.

Q So the Caftle was in darknefs?

A Yes.

COURT.   When you went from London to Barnet, was Bickley with you on the 10th of November.

A. Yes, he rode in the Hackney coach

Q Who were in the coach with Lady Strathmore?

A. Mr Bowes and Lucas—he got into the coach at Highgate.

Q Who came out of the coach in which Lady Strathmore was?

A Captain Farrer, as I underftand his name was

Q In the fecond coach there was Bickley.   Who drove the coach?

A I do not know—there was Bickley in the Hackney coach, and nobody elfe in the Hackney coach—I drove Mr. Prevot and the little man, whofe name I do not know, and Peacock, called Johnfon

Q And Mr Bowes came into your chaife before you got to Highgate?

A Yes—the middle of Highgate-hill, and Lucas got into the coach.

Q Did all the other three go into the Hackney coach then?

A Yes.

Q Was Lucas there?

A. Yes—he got into my Lady's carriage at Highgate; he went in the Hackney coach to Highgate—I faw Lucas firft at Highgate—I don't know that I faw him before I faw him at the Red Lion at Highgate.

Q. How he got to Highgate you do not know?

Mis BLAND *fworn.*

I have a houfe in Norfolk-ftreet, No 18. In October that houfe of mine was taken by a Gentleman, who did not mention any name—I afked of the fervant, and, as I underftood, his name was Colonel Meddifon or Morrifon—there were three gentlemen —I was not in the houfe—the Gentleman did not mention any name himfelf—he went there by that name—Mr Bowes is that Gentleman—there was a tall Gentleman, Mr. Peacock, he went by the name of Johnfon, I believe, he came about the 14th or 15th of October, they would have been a month on Monday —they went the 11th of November.

ROBERT CRUNDEL *fworn.*

I am footman to Lady Strathmore—I have lived with her above two years laft October—fhe lived in Bloomfbury-fquare.

Q Do you recollect at any time making obfervations of any thing that paffed in the fquare—of carriages with blinds up?

A Yes—I faw a carriage waiting the other fide of the fquare, I believe the blinds were up, the oppofite fide of the houfe—I was fent to fee whether there was anybody in it that I knew—I had my livery on, and the carriage drove on.

E

Q. Was

Q Was this in October?

A I do not recollect the time—I think it was

Q How long before Lady Strathmore was carried off?

A Better than a fortnight.

Q What day of the week was it?

A I believe it was on the Saturday—I am not sure.

Q Did you, in consequence of this, give any alarm?

A I told my Lady, when I came to the bottom of Southampton-street, I saw a person look out that I thought was Mr Bowes, and I told Lady Strathmore

Q What happened on the 10th of November?

A I went with Lady Strathmore that morning—Daniel Lee drove her.

Q Had he been a servant long, or lately come to her Ladyship?

A He had been some time, but not so long as me

Q Who was with her Ladyship in the carriage that day?

A There was one Mrs Morgan, a companion to my Lady, and Captain Farrer.

Q She keeps her Ladyship company?

A She does.

Q Was you molested by anybody?

A Yes we were—When we stopped in Oxford-street, at Mr Foster's, he is an iron-monger, as soon as we stopped there, one person came and took hold of me, and told me he would take me to prison for following a person about of the name of Cummins, and threatening to take his life away—I did not know any such person—I never had so threatened any body—that was a false charge—and before we set out, Edward Lucas came to our house, he said he had not seen anybody watching about, and he thought there was no call for the men to be continued—they had paid Lucas twelve shillings that morning—Lucas asked me whether Lady Strathmore was going out that morning—I told him I did not know—upon this I saw Lucas in Oxford-street, I thought he was come to protect Lady Strathmore—we were taken away and carried before one Mr. Justice Walker—as soon as ever Lucas came up he opened the coach-door, and took a pistol out of the carriage—Captain Farrer went into the house with Lady Strathmore and Mrs Morgan, and left his pistol in the coach—I had drawn up the blinds.

Q Who went with you?

A Daniel Lee—Nobody appeared against us, and we were all dismissed—this Cummins was the same man that went by the name of Charles Chapman—the constable pointed the man out to me, that was one Saunders, that was Chapman that I saw in this Court

Q At any time before this had you seen Bickley any where?

A Yes

Q When was that?

A I really do not know—I saw Prevot, Bickley, and another, get out of a coach—the carriage had been out to Chelsea—Lady Strathmore was not with it—they went down to the water—Prevot and Bickley hid themselves

Q How long was it before she was taken away?

A. A week, or better

Mr CHAMBRE Q. What was Mrs Morgan? Was not she a cook?

A. No, Sir, I do not know that she was.

Q Who was the person that threatened to take you before the Justice for threatening the life of one Cummins?

A. Meacham and Saunders

Q How was the person dressed you call Cummins?

A He was dressed in a green plush coat?

Q Did you see him afterwards in this coat?

A He was dressed in a black coat—I am sure he was the same person.

DANIEL LEE *sworn.*

I was coachman to Lady Strathmore—I saw coaches frequently about the square and other places, following her carriage

Q What was there particular about this carriage?

A Seeming to be pointing towards her Ladyship's house, the blinds were drawn up, apparently to me to be peeping through the little glasses, and likewise the glass

glass behind, I know Lucas the constable, I cannot tell you the day when he was first introduced, it might be eight or ten days before he was taken away, first he came to me about a fine dog that he had, that I believe was somewhere about the first of November, he began about observing the fastness of the doors being very strong, yes, sir, says I, We have need enough of it, he said, what was the matter? I told him then that there had been three people that I saw come up to the stable door, I followed them down, I saw three people a little bit before that, I cannot tell how many days they came down Little Russell-street, I followed them down, and saw them pointing up to the stable-door, which gave me great fear, that I would not go in that way, I was busy at work, and was telling him of a man whose name is Pritchard, stopping me in Holborn, says Lucas, should you know him again?—Yes, said I, I should.

Q In consequence of this conversation was Lucas employed by Lady Strath-more?

A He was

Q Was you present?

A No, I was not, this instrument Lucas gave me to protect the house, he told me he was employed to protect her ladyship, and the house, and he thought it his duty to do so, and he would to the utmost of his power, he came backwards and forwards after he undertook that office several times, I met him the day she was taken off at the Hole in the Wall, under a gateway—he says—Good morning to you, sir—Good morning to you, says I,—there was an additional watchman put on, and he says there is no occasion to continue that watchman, says I, I think not, that was on Friday morning the 10th of November, then he said he paid him two shillings a night, he could not give him less, and he discharged the man, and he was to be paid at Christmas very handsome for his trouble, he asked me if I was going out, I said I did not know—I went out afterwards with her Ladyship and was ordered to Mr Foster's in Oxford Road, there were Mrs. Morgan, her La-dyship, and Captain Farrer, her Ladyship got out, and immediately as she was out of the carriage Saunders the constable got up on my right hand on the box, I hit him on the hand, and bid him get down, I looked round to see that her lady-ship had got in safe—I bid him get down, he said, no, damn you, I will not get down, I have a warrant against you, and he shewed me the piece of paper, and I stopped, he took me and my fellow servant into custody—I did not see Lucas there at that time, they took us to the justice's, I saw Chapman there, I know him now, the Constables pointed to him as the man, I have seen him here since, he is the same man, I was carried to the justice's, nobody ever attended to charge me, I never saw Chapman before in my life.

Q What state was her Ladyship in at that time?

A She did not go out for six weeks and more, except twice to Westminster-Hall.

Q Was she able to get out of her carriage without help?

A. No, she was not

Court Q. Had you any conversation with Chapman when you were taken into custody?

A. Not a word

Q At the time he was by the horses?

A No, I asked him to take hold of the reins, he never said any thing that I heard, only I asked him to take hold of the reins.

WILLIAM SAUNDERS *sworn*

Q What are you?

A A Constable

Q Do you remember on the 9th of November last any application that Lucas made to you about any particular business?

A Yes, on the 9th of November, between eight and nine in the evening, one George Meacham came to me from him, I went to him, Lucas was in the parlour at the house he asked me if I should be busy to morrow, I told him I wanted to go to Smithfield, he told me says he if you will go along with me to-morrow I will give you a guinea on some particular business, and he said he would give Mea-

cham

cham a guinea to go with him, Lucas called for some punch, and we drank, I was to meet him the next morning at Harwood's, I went the next morning and knocked at the door, and in came Lucas, says he, Saunders come over to Smith's at the Yorkshire Grey, that is in Hart-street, Bloomsbury, accordingly I went with Lucas to Smith's, at the Yorkshire Grey—I went up stairs, and who should I see but this little coachman Broad, Lucas asked us to have something to drink that morning, we had a pint of purl, Meacham was not there, says Lucas damn it why does not Meacham come, presently Meacham came to the corner of Hide-Street, Lucas threw up the window and beckoned him, accordingly he came up stairs, Lucas went backwards and forwards about the room, and began to damn and swear that the other people did not come, presently there was a coach came out of Holborn in Lion-Street, so presently he goes down and John Cummins comes up for one, says Lucas I am glad you are come, so Lucas and he went to the farther part of the room, they came back again, says Lucas, Mr. Saunders this man has got a warrant, (pointing to Chapman) Lucas gave me the warrant to look at, I looked at it *(here the witness read the warrant)* This is the warrant. Lucas took the warrant back again and walked up and down the room two or three times backwards and forwards, and presently goes and calls a hackney coach, between twelve and one a coach passed, says Lucas, come down we are all ready my boys, this man Meacham, Cummins, Lucas, a little man and me got in, now says Lucas drive on as fast as you can and every corner you come to halt a little

Q Did you pursue in this hackney coach Lady Strathmore's coach?

A We went up as far as the Pantheon, Lucas gave me the warrant, so when we got out of the coach, I said to Chapman be so kind as to shew me the prisoners, says Chapman that coachman (pointing to my Lady's coachman) and the footman, so I went to him and said how do you do coachman, says he, get down, damn it my Lady is just gone into that house, so I told him I had a warrant and I called upon Meacham to assist me in the King's name, and he did and put them into a hackney coach, we desired Cummins to come to the office directly, he said he would, we went to Mr Walker's office and took the prisoners there, but Cummins did not come, and they were discharged, we waited there a quarter of an hour.

MR. JUSTICE WALKER *sworn, (looks at the warrant)*.

That is my warrant, it was granted upon an information laid before me.

MR GARROW. Q Did you take any information in writing, Sir?

A No farther than that there was a complaint made before me by one John Cummins, I asked him whether he was sure he was afraid, his answer was he was sure, for it was time for him to be afraid as he stood with a pistol at his head, I have known Lucas some years, he attended my office at that time.

MRS. MORGAN *sworn*.

Q. You are acquainted with Lady Strathmore?

A. Yes.

Q Do you recollect one Lucas previous to the time she was taken away, have you seen him and spoke to him?

A. Yes

Q Had he been employed by Lady Strathmore for any purpose and what?

A. For the purpose of guarding her Ladyship's house, on the 10th of November I went out with Lady Strathmore, on that day I did not see him till I saw him at Mr Foster's.

Q Who was in the coach with Lady Strathmore and you?

A Captain Farrer, he had a pistol with him, by the desire of Lady Strathmore we went to Mr Foster's in Oxford-Street, we went up stairs into the room and locked ourselves in, because we saw a mob round the door, and saw somebody lay hold of the coachman and footman. while we were in that state Lucas came to the door, he called out my dear Lady here is Lucas your friend, let me in, the door was fast, he was let in by one of us, he told Lady Strathmore not to be afraid for there was a hundred people after her, and they had taken away her coachman and footman, and she might depend upon it at the peril of his life he would take care of her, in consequence of this she went down stairs with Lucas, he had hold of Lady Strath-

more's

more's arm, he faid nothing to me then, when we got down ftairs he faid Lady Strathmore was his prifoner, he did not fay then what for, but immediately after he faid he had a warrant againft her fhe was exceedingly alarmed, I then faid myfelf to Lucas, can you feize a countefs as you can a common perfon? fome more words paffed, Lucas faid it was at the peril of his life and fhe muft go with him, I then faid Mr Lucas tnen why did not you let Lady Strathmore know this, and he faid upon my foul I did not know it five minutes before, I undoubtedly thought him the friend—he had been paid twelve fhillings that morning   Mr Lucas told me there was a warrant alfo for me, and the beft thing I could do was to make my efcape, I then afked him if I might not be permitted to fpeak to Lady Strathmore—he faid, yes—I then told Lady Strathmore I would go out the back way, and fend Mr Lacey to her, the Attorney—I went away foon after.

Q Did you fee her Ladyfhip foon afte.?

A I faw her on her arrival

Q What condition was fhe in?

A. I can fcarcely defcribe her condition, fhe was fo altered, fo full of mud, and dreffed in an old bed gown—I have kept the cloaths fhe had on ever fince (*a red petticoat, a coloured apron, an old bed gown, and an old bonnet produced*) that was the drefs fhe came home in

Q Did you examine her perfon, to fee if there were any marks of violence about her?

A She fhewed me her breaft, there were feveral black marks and bruifes on her breaft, and one of her temples was difcoloured with marks and bruifes.

Q. Was you prefent at the time the articles were drawn?

A. Yes.

Q What condition was fhe in?

A. She was fo feeble fhe could not write, but dictated

Mr FIELDING Q. How long have you lived in the fervice of Lady Strathmore?

A Since the 18th of May, 1784.

Q What capacity did you firft come into the fervice?

A As her woman

Q And have fo continued till this time?

A. Yes

Q Has Lady Strathmore been vifited by many Ladies of late, within the laft twelve months?

A By feveral.

Q You are pretty much in her intimacy and company?

A I have been.

Q. Is it the cuftom for you to be in company with her the moft part of the day?

A Yes

Q Is it the cuftom for you to be in the fame room with her at reft?

A I fleep in the next room to her, with the room door open

Q Does any body lay in the room with Lady Strathmore?

A Not in the room

Q There is nobody but yourfelf in that room that adjoins?

A No the door is always open

Q You had an opportunity of knowing pretty much the ftate of Lady Strathmore's mind, and the ftate of her fpirits for the laft twelve months?

A Yes.

Q Have you taken her to be regular in conducting herfelf, does fhe feem to have the command of her reafon?

A I think fhe has a very good command of her mind—I do not know any Lady that has fo much poffeffion of her mind

Q Then I am going to afk a very ftrange fort of a queftion—if that be the cafe, you will inform me, whether my fuggeftion has any fort of foundation, has fhe ever thought of treating with conjurors or forcerers?

A I do not believe there is fuch a thing as a conjuror

Q Have you ever had any converfation between you about there being fuch a being that can foretell human events?

A. I do not believe there are any fuch.

Q Did you ever hint to her that there are fuch people as fortune-tellers.

F

A There

A. There was a circumstance, that Mr. Bowes had loft a diamond ring, and a man was accufed of it, and I faid to this man, I wifh I was in England, merely to fee whether I could collect any thing from his countenance, fays I to him, there are fuch people in England that could make people bring the ring and lay it on the table.

Q. Then you yourfelf have a little faith in thefe people about fortune-telling?

COURT. Q Can this be material any way in the world.

A Yes, my Lord, in a matter that may come on hereafter in this profecution.

Mr ERSKINE. Q As far as fhe has fpoke, it certainly is not mate.ial

Mr. FIELDING. Q I have been difappointed in what I expected—have you known the ftate of Lady Strathmore's expences of late?

A Yes.

Q Is fhe in debt?

A She has nothing of her own, and confequently muft be in debt.

Q Has it happened to you to know the amount of her debts?

A I can tell pretty nearly.

Q To what amount are her debts in the laft two years?

Mr MINGAY I object to this—Does your Lordfhip think it is material, or re-levant, or admiffable evidence, for this Lady to be crofs-examined about it.

COURT The Court muft rely on the candour of the Council, that they will not afk queftions that are improper, if the Gentlemen think fo

Mr FIELDING. I take it for granted, that part of Mr. Bowes's defence will be, that there has been a confiderable degree of extravagance

COURT Then I am decidedly of opinion for rejecting the evidence, if it is not material in this trial you fhall not have liberty to put the queftion

Mr. ERSKINE I am fure, hitherto, your Lordfhip can have had no reafon to complain of our deviation, if on the part of this profecution thofe mere naked circumftances which go to the conviction of the defendant, or of all the defendants, upon all the counts, were fingly relied upon by my learned friend—if they did not go into the matter of extreme aggravation, perhaps a good many of the queftions now about to be afked, might be fpared, but as the motive of Mr Bowes for confpiring with others to feize the perfon of Lady Strathmore is very material in this iffue, and as there are fome occafions that juftify a hufband in taking his wife, though perhaps none in thofe circumftances of violence that have been hitherto proved, but which the Court can-not take it for granted that they will not be contradicted, whether it was not legal in them to feize her perfon, though not accompanied with thofe acts of terror and vio-lence that have been introduced into the cafe, for if this cafe fhould be ftripped of all the aggravations, and leaving it nakedly to this point, that a hufband in the courfe of doing a legal act, has conducted himfelf illegally—I am not difpofed to go out of the cafe, I only want to know the way in which Lady Strathmore was living at the time Mr Bowes conceived this idea

COURT I cannot think it ftrikes me at all applicable to this cafe

Mr FIELDING Q Captain Farrer had been in the habit of going broad with this Lady as her guard—he has called on her frequently, and has carried arms?

A Yes

Q, How long has the acquaintance been between Lady Strathmore and Captain Farrer?

A Captain Farrer has known Lady Strathmore from her childhood, and her Lady-fhip's family from his infancy

EDWARD CROOKE *fworn.*

Mr GARROW Q You keep the Pyed Bull in Little Ruffel Street?

A Yes, clofe by Lady Strathmore's ftables

Q Do you know this Gentleman? *(pointing to Mr. Bowes)*

A Yes, I have feen him.

Q Have you feen Peacock?

A. No, Sir, I faw Mr Bowes.

Q Perhaps you know him by fome other name?

A No, Sir, I faw this Gentleman at the Crown and Anchor, there were three gentlemen came to our houfe one night, one in a failor's drefs, the others I do not know what drefs, like gentlemens fervant's—they called for a pot of beer—they came on foot, I do not know who they were, after that they called for a shilling's worth of gin and water

Q. What did you do in consequence of their calling?

A If I do not begin at the first I cannot go on——they wanted to sleep all night, I told them I had no lodging, they asked if they could dine there the next day, I told them they might, they said bread and cheese would serve them, a hackney coach came the next day with three men in it

Q Who came on the second day?

A. I cannot tell.

Q How were they dressed?

A I cannot tell I am sure, they enquired if any persons had been at the house the night before, I told them there were, they said they had been robbed at some place or other, and that they had a lodging somewhere about there, and would be glad to have them taken up, I told the gentlemen in the coach they wanted to lodge with me, they said they wished they had

Q Did these people in the coach make any appointment with you to go to Norfolk-street

A. They did

Q What was you to go to Norfolk-street for?

A. They told me to come down to the Crown and Anchor in the Strand, and to ask for the Justice to-morrow morning, and to clean myself, accordingly I went to the Crown and Anchor, but I went first to speak to Mr. Lucas, he was not with them at the time, I told Mr. Lucas there were three gentlemen after the men that had been at our house the night before, and I supposed that there had been some robbery.

Q. Where did you see Lucas?

A. At his own house, Lucas said, tell the gentleman that I belong to the office, and if they want any body taken up, I will do it, so I told him I would tell them, then I went to the Crown and Anchor and asked for the Justice, the gentlewoman shewed me into the parlour, there were three gentlemen——I do not know who they were——I believe Mr Bowes was one of them.

Q How was he dressed.

A. I cannot tell, I do not remember whether he had his own hair or a wig, I have known Lucas two or three years before.

Q Have you seen him lately?

A. I came here with him this morning

Q. When did you see Mr Bowes last?

A I do not know, I have not seen him since, I cannot tell whether I have seen him or not.

Q Have not you seen him within this week?

A. I cannot tell I am sure, I think I saw Mr. Bowes a little while ago at Mr. Lucas's

Mr. MINGAY. Go along, I will not ask you another Question

Captain FARRER, *sworn.*

Mr LAW. Q I believe you have seen Lucas before the 10th of November?

A Yes, sir, I visit at Lady Strathmore's

Q Did you see him in company with Lady Strathmore?

A Yes

Q. Do you know in what situation he was?

A I understood he was employed to detect people that were lurking about the house, on the 10th of November I went out in the morning of that day with Lady Strathmore, she signified a desire to go out an airing, but was apprehensive of so doing, as she heard Mr Bowes intended seizing her, we went to Mr Foster's in Oxford-street, when we got there on stopping at the door there were a number of people surrounded the place, Lady Strathmore and Mrs. Morgan went into the shop of Foster, and I followed her, and Lucas came after, there were some men, which I supposed to be constables, who took the coachman and footman away under a warrant.

Q Did you go into the house then?

A. I went

A I went into the fhop of Mr Fofter, and Lady Strathmore and Mrs. Morgan ran up ftairs, there is a door which communicates into the fhop, I faw Lucas knocking at that door, I heard him fay my lady do not be alarmed, here is Lucas your friend, I do not immediately know whether the door was opened, upon that I went out immediately to fee what was become of the coachman and footman, when I returned I faw Lady Strathmore and Mrs Morgan come down with Lucas, her Ladyfhip continued in the fhop in very great agitation and fear, refpecting this bufinefs, then Lucas faid he had a warrant for her, that he would protect her Ladyfhip to the utmoft of his power, he faid he was to carry her to the Juftices.

Q Who had got poffeffion then of Lady Strathmore's coach?

A. When I went out there was a man of the name of Broad that was on the coach box, I afked him what ne did there, and if he took poffeffion of the coach? He told me I fhould know, Lady Strathmore was in very great agitation, and was treated very rudely by this man Lucas, who had hold of her arm, and at laft he pulled out a conftable's ftaff, and faid, by God, my Lady, you are my prifoner, and at the peril of my life I muft take you, he put her into the coach, and told Mrs. Morgan to take care of herfelf, for there was a warrant out againft her, Lady Strathmore objected going into the coach, unlefs I went with her, and in confequence of that Lucas faid to me, fir, I call upon you in the king's name to aid and affift me, I got into the carriage with Lady Strathmore, and Lucas with me, the carriage drove down Oxford-ftreet to Tottenham-Court Turnpike, Broad drove it —I remember a chaife ftanding at the Turnpike Gate—I do not know the driver, I did not take particular notice of him, but I fince learned it was Peter Orme, we went then to Highgate, Lucas, me, and Lady Strathmore in the carriage, Lucas on the road faid there would be terrible work, and he was afraid fome lives would be loft, going through Kentifh Town I told him if that was like to be the cafe it would be proper to raife people to affift and refift force by force, he faid, fir, you had better go to Highgate, when we got to Highgate, I got out of the carriage, I went into a room with Lady Strathmore and Lucas, fhe was much frightened, and looking round I faw Mr Bowes, Lucas talked of going to Lord Manffield's, when Lady Strathmore faw Mr Bowes fhe was amazingly alarmed, as much fo as a woman could be, fhe cried out, the window was thrown up by her, fhe cried out murder repeatedly, Mr Bowes when he came into the room afked me who I was, I told him I was a gentleman, fir, fays he, this is my wife, I went out of the door, with intent to raife people to relieve her, in confequence of which, after I had done my endeavours, I came near the houfe, and Mr. Bowes in perfon came out to me and faid, fir, if you do not be quiet I will knock you down, I faid, Mr Bowes remember what you have faid, Mr Bowes, like a man of very great courage, faid, fir I will give you fatisfaction, I did not think myfelf bound as a gentleman to take notice of Mr. Bowes, there was very great confufion in the place, I faw Lady Strathmore at the window, calling out murder, and for help, how fhe came out of the houfe I do not know, I went into the carriage with her, fhe pulled me up ftep by ftep, after her, I was confidering what was beft to be done, I accordingly got in with Lady Strathmore and Mr. Bowes, and Mr. Lucas got into the fame carriage, but in going down Highgate-Hill Lady Strathmore got up and feemed to be very much alarmed, fhe obferved it was not the way to Lord Manffield's, I faid, my Lady, I believe it is not, to which Mr. Bowes faid, fir, hold your tongue, or elfe I will turn you out of the carriage, Lady Strathmore had hold of my arm, fays he, damn you, madam, are not you afhamed of yourfelf, when your daughter lays dying, upon going a little farther he very politely faid, fir, if you pleafe you may get out of the carriage, I accepted of his polite offer, I thought I could be of no fervice with the number of men, I faw no other people armed, and from Lucas's declarations at different times that he would blow Mr Bowes's brains out, I concluded he had arms, I got out, I made the alarm and followed

Q At firft you did apprehend you were going to Lord Manffield's?

A Yes, I did, I did not immediately recollect the circumftance.

Q I need not afk you whether this was by her confent or without her confent?

A. It was too apparent to every body.

EDWARD

EDWARD BROAD *sworn.*

Q. Are you the coachman that was hired?

A. Yes, Sir.

Q. Who hired you?

A. Lucas.

Q. You are a hackney coachman?

A. Yes, I was hired by Lucas the 9th of November, I am the person that went to Foster's in Oxford-Street, I was employed by Lucas to go there, I did not see Bickley till I came to Highgate

Q. Had you any conversation with him?

A. I saw a stage that had stopped at the Red Lion door, and seeing him at the Red Lion door I asked him if he had been in the country, he said he had, I saw him no more till I came to Barnet.

Q. What did Bickley say?

A. He said it was Lady Strathmore, and that Mr. Bowes was her husband, that he had a law-suit depending in some court, and that he must have Lady Strathmore in his possession at the time the cause was coming on, he told me this at the Red Lion at Barnet.

Mr. MINGAY. Q. Did you learn from Bickley how long he had been in the service of Mr Bowes?

A. He said he had been employed by Mr. Bowes for three weeks and had two guineas a week.

WILLIAM BROUGHTON *sworn.*

Mr. GARROW. Q. Where do you live?

A. I keep the Red Lion at Barnet, I remember very well Lady Strathmore being brought to my house, I saw Mr. Bowes, Lady Strathmore and Lucas in my Lady's coach, I was standing in the yard, and there came in a man who I found afterwards was Peacock, he came forwards and ordered four horses to go down the hill to bring the coach up, I was anxious I thought it was a run away match to Gretna-Green; as I was coming out of my gate some body said these are Mr. Bowes's, when I came the coach was arrived with a pair of horses, while I was anxious of getting the horses put to it there was a gentleman said it was Lady Strathmore, so I never went to the coach, I thought it would be imprudent to look into the coach, at last I saw Lady Strathmore, a man in spectacles, whom I afterwards found was Lucas, and Mr. Bowes, all at once my Lady Strathmore jumped up and called out murder, murder, help for god sake, murder, murder, with that the man Lucas got up and laid hold of her hands and pressed her down in the carriage, and I really thought my Lady in struggling would have broke the glasses, instantly they drove away.

Q. How did the rest of the people get from your house?

A. There was a post-chaise and pair, and I believe Peacock and somebody went in, I did not look much at them, I saw they looked like rogues, she called at my house coming back and was an object of pity she was, she called out put four horses, I saw a woman in a bonnet and an old handkerchief like a woman that was sifting cinders in Grays-Inn-Lane.——Orme has since been in my service.

Q. Do you know from your own knowledge of any application made to him by these defendants?

A. I know nothing but what he told me himself.

EMANUEL MENIER *sworn.*

I was there when the carriage came up on the 10th of November, there was a man which was Mr. Lucas, I recollected Lady Strathmore, and told Mr. Broughton so immediately, I saw Lucas force her Ladyship down in the carriage, and she let down the glasses and cried murder, help, and assistance for godsake in the struggle putting the glasses up she put her hand upon it and broke it, she afterwards went on.

G

Mr ERSKINE

Mr. Erskine. Q. Then at this cry of murder, and being forced down by a man in spectacles in the coach, you was present besides Broughton?

A. There were other people present, Sir—there was a tall gentleman, who I believe is Peacock.

Q. How came you to suffer a carriage, conducted in that way, to go from the door?

A. The reason was, I happened to mention it to one Cass, and he said, if I mentioned a word I should be murdered by some of the parties.

Broughton. It was done so momentary, I had not time, but I immediately took advice what to do, and sent express to London.

Mr. Mingay. Now I will call a witness who saw her at Stilton, and saw him offer her the papers, and her refusal of it.

WILLIAM BARKER *sworn*.

I live at the Bell at Stilton—I know Mr Bowes—I recollect him coming there on the 10th of November—My Lady's coach came first and a chaise after.

Q. Who was in that coach?

A. I did not observe—the lady got out.

Q. Do you recollect any thing that passed between Mr Bowes and her Ladyship?

A. Yes—they went into a room—Mr. Bowes asked for pen, ink and paper, which accordingly carried—after he sat down I saw him writing—after I went in he was standing up by the side of the lady—what he said I cannot say, but, as soon as I got into the room and shut the door, I heard my Lady say, I will not sign it for you nor any body, upon which I went out—as soon as I got into the kitchen she was hallooing out murder—I saw her pushed into the carriage myself, either by Bowes or Lucas—It was very late at night—it was twelve o'clock—her cap almost knocked off her head—She then called murder, murder, is there nobody to assist me?—She did not get into the same carriage she went first, and there were two or three people in the hind carriage, and somebody said, Bundle out, bundle out, and he forced my Lady into the hind chaise—her coach went on, and I believe Mr. Bowes got in, and when she cried out is there nobody to assist me, yes? says the Gentleman in spectacles, I will assist you—I will jump up behind.

Mr. Chambre. Q. When you heard this conversation there was nobody present but Mr Bowes and Lady Strathmore?

A. No.

Q. You were without the door?

A. No—I was within the room and had shut too the door?

Q. Whilst Lady Strathmore staid at your house at Stilton, were any of the maids with her?

Y. Yes—I believe Mr. Bowes ordered one of the maids in, because he would not let her go up stairs—my Lady frightened the maid very much—she was a poor innocent girl, she was not the chambermaid.

JOHN THACKER *sworn*.

I am hostler at the Bell at Stilton, I saw Lady Strathmore there between the 10th and 11th of November, she was running up the street, passing the carriage, she cried out murder—she called for help.

Q. What did the people say that got her again?

A. They said, Get out of that chaise, and put her in the last chaise—some people said to one another, Here she is—assist me and put her in the last chaise—she cried out murder—they got her again and put her in the last chaise—one of them forced her in, I think he had spectacles on—they almost pulled off her cap with the top of the chaise.

THOMAS WADE *sworn*.

I drove Mr. Bowes from Greta-Bridge to Streatlam-Castle—they called me up, I cannot tell the time, they told me it was Lady Bowes and Mr. Bowes—I cannot exactly tell the time we got there—she was in the carriage before I was ready.

Q. Did any thing pass on the journey?

A. Nothing at all particular—as soon as she got out of the carriage she cried out several times, I am brought here by force, and desire it may be made public—there were
thre

three in a chaife behind—I do not know who they were—I faw one fince that I know very well.

Q. A young man?

A He is

Q Snould you know his name if it was mentioned ?

A. I did not hear his name—I did not ftay long at Streatlam-Caftle—I had fome converfation with Mr. Bourn—he faid, he fuppofed I had liked to have overturned the carriage, and that made her cry out fo—I told him, that was impoffible, becaufe fhe never cried out till fhe got out of the carriage—Mr Bourn afked what it was fhe did cry out for—I told him, very like he might know as well as me, or fomething to that effect— we were not long there—Mr Bowes's fervant paid me, and Bourn gave me fome drink —I faw them them take out fome fire-arms out of the hindmoft chaife, I think they were piftols—it was in the dead of the night

Mr ERSKINE   Q You fay Lady Strathmore got out of the carriage and walked into the houfe?

A. Yes.

Q Mr. Bowes attended her ?

A Yes—as foon as it ftopped fhe got out of the carriage and went into the Caftle —Mr. Bowes took hold of her and they went together—I never faw her Ladyfhip afterwards.

Q When was it that Lady Strathmore cried out that fhe was there by force, and defired it might be public ?

A As foon as fhe got out of the carriage

Mr. MINGAY.   My Lord, now we are going as to Thomas Bowes

THOMAS COLPITS *fworn.*

I live at Cockfield, about five miles from Streatlam—I know Lady Strathmore and her family very well—I was at Barnard-Caftle on the 25th of October, and I was coming along, and obferved Mr Bowes, Mr Bourn and Prevot, mount their horfes and proceed toward Streatlam—after they had been gone a fufficient time to get to Streatlam and further, Mr Bourn returned to Mr. Hobfon's houfe—then Mr. Bourn went to the Poft-houfe, and gave out that Mr Bowes had received a very bad accident on the road—that his horfe had fallen, and that he had pitched over him, two or three times—I was fufpicious that it was fome trick, they play fo many—I took my horfe immediately, with another perfon, and rode on as faft as I could—I came up to them and faw Mr Bowes laying near the turnpike, apparently dead, with his head on a heap of ftones, and a little hay under him—Prevot had his hand behind him, and was holding his arm—Mr Hobfon was by him, and two other perfons, they were tying up his arm—I underftood then he was blooded.

Q Was Prevot fo near that he could hear, or Bowes ?

A. They were within two or three yards.

Q What was faid ?

A That he had broke three ribs, that the blood was coming out of his ears—that Mr Hobfon fuppofed his fhoulder was out, and his head was much bruifed—a little while after Bourn came back with a poft-chaife and took the money out of his pockets; at which Prevot retired a little way off and counted it—it was almoft dark, and in five minutes or lefs. they counted to the amount of fourteen hundred pounds—I heard them gingle the money into their hands—Bourn was for looking over the Bank-bills—They told the people, particularly Mr. Hobfon, to take notice there were 1400l.—After he had lain a little while they put him in the chaife—Bourn and Hobfon got in, and went to Streatlam-Caftle.

Q. Was this known publicly afterwards ?

A. Yes—A great deal of pains was taken to fpread it ?

ROBERT HOBSON *fworn*

I am a furgeon at Barnard-Caftle, on Tuefday the 24th of October laft, Mr. Bourn, who was Mr Bowes's agent, came to my houfe, and defired me to take a ride over to Streatlam, that he, Mr. Bowes, wanted to fee me—after ftaying fome time, he faid, I have a fecret to truft you with—can you keep a fecret ?—fays I, what fecret ?—then Mr. Bowes began, and faid to me, Sir, the fituation of my affairs are fuch, that I wifh to be fecreted for a while, for

for I am afraid some trouble is coming upon me—says he, the secret is this, I will fall off my horse to morrow, between Streatlam Castle and Barnard-Castle, you will be sent for, and you must say I have fallen off my horse, and have broke three of my ribs— you must attend me at the Castle the next morning—I did so, and I went again on the Friday-morning, and when I came there on the 6th of November, Mr. Bourn informed me that Mr Bowes was gone off in the night, for, says he, all the people in Streatlam Castle know my motions and movements.

Mr Law I believe, in consequence of this, you communicated it to several people?

A Yes.

Q I believe to the respectable gentleman in Court?

A Yes

Q Did you inform any gentlemen in the neighbourhood?

A I told everybody it was so.

Q. Did you tell Mr. Lee so?

A. Mr Bowes had wrote a Letter to Mr Lee, which he desired me to copy.

Q I believe you represented that Mr Bowes was very resigned to this cala- mity?

A. Mr. Bowes said, Mr Hobson, be so kind as to copy this for Mr Lee—says I, Mr. Lee will never forgive me, if I tell him a lie and he finds it out—Oh, says he, never mind, I'll make that up with him—I attended there backwards and forwards for ten days or a fortnight—I rode there every day, and I acquainted every body, by his desire, that he was so bad as not to be seen—I went over there one morning and I saw Bourn, and he said he had a letter for Mr. Bowes—says I, where is he—says he, in London—says I, the devil! what does he do there—I did not know he was gone to London.

Q. You attended him only two days?

A. Yes.

Q. And sent medicines for ten days?

A. Yes

Q. Bourn was there, and saw that he had not had this accident?

A Yes.

Q Did you see Mr Thomas Bowes there at that time?

A. He came there once or twice, if not three times; Mr. Bourn and he had some conversation together, and Mr Bowes

Mr. Erskine. Q Mr Bowes told you in general terms, that he had a very particular reason why he wished to be concealed from his friends?

A. Yes, he did—that he was afraid of bailiffs.

Q Mr Bowes imposed upon you?

A. He did.

Q. He did not give you the smallest reason to suppose, that he wished this sham sickness should be put on that he might get away to London, for the purpose of carry- ing away Lady Strathmore?

A. Not in the least.

Q. You thinking that it was a good natured action to give this gentleman an op- portunity of treating them in this way, under the sham of sickness, you agreed to come the next day?

A. Yes.

Q You had not the least conception of this plan?

A. Not the least

Q. I ask you as an honest man, had you any reason to know and believe, that this gentleman, Mr. Bowes, did not impose on Mr. Thomas Bowes, as he did on you?

A. I sincerely believe Mr. Thomas Bowes knew nothing of Mr. Bowes's plan—he came on business twice—he said he wanted to see Mr Bowes on particular business— Bourn told him he could not be seen, and Bourn carried up the message—I believe he was quite in the dark about it

Q I believe you yourself brought down a verbal answer, in order to deceive him?

A I did

Q. That is your honest opinion on the subject of Mr. Thomas Bowes?

A Yes

Q. You knew it was a sham illness as well as Bourn?

A. Yes—I had no reason to believe that Bourn was imposed on.

Mr.

Mr. ERSKINE. Q. You say that Mr Bourn told you afterwards that he was gone to London?

A. Yes, that was either the fifth or sixth of November

Q. Did not he tell you so with all the appearances of surprize?

A. I do not know, he had a letter in his hand, which he read, and says he, I have a letter from Mr Bowes in London—in consequence of this message passing backwards and forwards, I do not believe Thomas Bowes was acquainted with the subject of the sham fall.

THOMAS RIPPON *sworn*.

I was writer to Mr Thomas Bowes one month within two or three days—I remember his going to Streatlam Castle

Q. How was he dressed?

A. I cannot tell

Q. Had he a great coat on, or had he not?

A. He had.

Q. Was it his own—one that he usually wore?

A. Yes.

Q. When did he return to Streatlam Castle

A. On the Thursday night.

Q. Have you ever seen the great coat that Lady Strathmore returned in?

A. Yes.

Q. Is it very like the great coat Mr Bowes generally wore?

A. I think it is—I was the person that usually enquired for letters for Thomas Bowes

Q. Had you any particular directions about the time of the fall, from Mr. Thomas Bowes, respecting his letters

A. He ordered me to go every morning as soon as I got up, to the post-house, to ask for his letters, for he expected letters from Mr A.R Bowes—he did not tell me from what place he expected them

Q. Would the letters come by that conveyance, if they had been written at Streatlam Castle?

A. They might come that way, but they generally come by an old man named Christopher Stokel, and not by the general post

Q. Was there any thing particular in the manner in which Mr. Bowes did his business about that time?

A. Within two or three days of the time when I heard Lady Strathmore was carried off, I had not access to his office as usual, he locked the door—he did not use to lock it till then, if he locked the door in the former part of the time I lived with him, I had access to the key—I had not during this time

Mr CHAMBRE. Q. How long have you lived with Mr Bowes, before this time that he went to the Castle?

A. About three weeks

Q. Was not he concerned for him in a great deal of business?

A. Yes.

Q. Was not there some law processes against Mr Bowes?

A. There was.

Q. Was there not a process out in that cause

Mr. MINGAY. I object—do you know that there was such business going on at that time—do you know that there was business of that sort going on?

A. I do not know—I have no knowledge at all of any—I was employed merely as writer and servant

Q. How long before that did Mr Thomas Bowes give you notice to quit his service?

A. Not till Saturday the 18th of November—he gave me no notice till he paid me off—it was Saturday the 18th of November

Q. Did you give Mr. Bowes any notice?

A. No.

H

RIDGWAT

——— Ridgway *sworn*.

I am Tipſtaff—I arrived at Streatlam Caſtle on the 13th of November.

Q. What time of the day ?

A. About three—I could not get admittance—I called out, a gentleman came to the door—I knocked at the door, a gentleman anſwered me—Who do you want ?—I ſaid, I want to ſpeak to Mr. Bowes—ſays he, Who are you—ſays I, my name is Ridgway, I am alone—he ſaid, I cannot open the door—open the window, Sir, ſays I, open the window—he opened the window, and I ſpoke to him—I underſtand him ſince to be Mr. Thomas Bowes, that is the gentleman, I aſked him if Mr. Bowes was there, he ſaid, no—ſays I, how long has he been gone—ſays he, I cannot hold any converſation with you on the ſubject, or words to that effect—I waited there a long while—I ſhoved the rules under the door, and there I left them—I called out at the ſame time, Mr. Andrew Robinſon Bowes, I have ſhoved a Habeas Corpus, and a copy of the original rule under the door, and I deem it a good ſervice—I called ſo a vaſt number of times—I demanded Lady Strathmore a vaſt number of times, by me and a conſiderable number of people

Mr Erskine Q. There were a conſiderable number of people ſurrounding the Caſtle when you held this converſation with Mr. Thomas Bowes ?

A. There was afterwards.

Q. How long after ?

A. Ten minutes

Q. Then they muſt be near the Caſtle ?

A. I cannot ſay

Q. Could it be otherwiſe—as ſoon as Thomas Bowes opened the window, and you aſked him if Mr. Andrew Robinſon Bowes was gone, he ſhut the window and ſaid he could hold no converſation with you ?

A. Yes, then the Caſtle was ſurrounded, though at a great diſtance, by a great number of people, they might be two hundred yards behind a row of trees, the people were very violent, I deſired them to deſiſt

Q. It muſt have given ſome alarm to the people in the Caſtle ?

A. No doubt, Sir.

Mr. Mingay. Q. When you firſt called out, and before you put the papers under the door, was Thomas Bowes within hearing then ?

A. I think he muſt

Q. Was the croud of people near you then ?

A. I ſuppoſe not leſs than fifty people ſurrounded, and ſaw me put the papers under the door

Mr. Erskine Q. Did you ſee the perſon of Mr. Thomas Bowes after that time ?

A. Not to ſwear to

Q. Then how far back he retired from the window you cannot tell ?

A. No

Q. There was a conſiderable number of people round you ?

A. Yes.

Q. Can you take upon you to ſwear with any degree of poſitiveneſs, whether he heard you or no ?

A. I ſhall not attempt to ſwear it, I think it was poſſible he might.

Mr Mingay Q. Was it impoſſible but he muſt hear you ?

A. I think it was not impoſſible.

Mr. Erskine. Q. On what day.

A. On the 13th.

Q. (*To Mr Hobſon*) Did not you tell Mr. Bowes juſt before Mr. Ridgway came up, that there was a bailiff at the door ?

A. I went to viſit Mr. Bowes and my Lady, I was going round to the back door, and Mr Bowes opened the front door to me—there was a man came paſt, ſays Mr. Thomas Bowes, who is that, ſays I, he is a bailiff.

Mr. Mingay. Q. What time was this ?

A. It was on Monday, Mr. Thomas Bowes was at the Caſtle, he opened the door, I was there about ten—it was before Ridgway came.

CHRISTOPHER

CHRISTOPHER STOKEL, *sworn.*

I carried a letter from Streatlam Castle to Darlington on Sunday the 12th of November from Mr Bowes.

A I delivered it to Mr. Bowes at Darlington, it was towards night.

Q. Did you carry a letter on the 25th of October?

A. I cannot tell.

Q Was that the day that it was reported that Mr. Bowes had fallen from his horse?

A I carried one that day.

Q Who was it from?

A I carried it from Streatlam Castle, I believe Mr. Bourn gave me a letter to carry, and I delivered it to Mr Bowes at Darlington, I saw Mr. Bowes of Darlington at Streatlam Castle on the day that Mr. Bowes was reported to have fallen from his horse.

Mr. ERSKINE. Q Now old man, now that you are out of your training, let us see what you have said to this gentleman, tell your own story, without Mr. Law holding up your chin?

A. I carried a letter from Mr Bourn to Mr. Bowes, they were both together, I do not know who wrote the letter, it was the day he fell from his horse, I carried bank notes, which I gave to Mr. Thomas Bowes at Darlington, and he gave me cash for them

Q What day was that?

A. The day he fell.

Q Did you bring back any money?

A. I brought back a parcel.

Q. Did you carry the notes to get cash for?

A. Yes

Q. What day was it you carried these notes?

A. It was on a Wednesday

Q Was that the day Mr. Bowes was supposed to fall from his horse?

A. Yes.

Q. What were the notes that you carried?

A I brought back threescore guineas from Mr Thomas Bowes

Mr. LAW Q Now I will ask you did you receive any notes whatever, bank or other, from Mr Bowes of Streatlam Castle?

A. No, I carried a letter.

Q. From whom did you receive the notes you got changed into cash?

A Thomas Bowes of Darlington he gave me notes to get changed, and I got them changed.

Mr. ERSKINE Q Did you see Mr. Thomas Bowes open the letter?

A No, I did not

Q But he gave you money in return for the letter?

A. Yes, I gave the cash to Mr. Thomas Bowes.

JAMES FARRER, *Esq. sworn.*

Mr. MINGAY. Be so good as to acquaint the Court and Jury what you know of this matter?

A. Being in the North, I had an express sent me to Carlisle, acquainting me that Mr Bowes had forcible seized the Countess of Strathmore, and had taken her to Streatlam Castle, whereupon I immediately set off for that place, and arrived there about noon, as near as I can recollect, the Wednesday following the 15th November.

Q What time of the day was it?

A I think it was about twelve or one.

Q When you got there was there any croud?

A. There was a good many people, I know Mr. Thomas Bowes of Darlington, I never had any particular acquaintance with him—I know he is an Attorney living at Darlington, I have known him act for Mr. A. R. Bowes.

Q When you came to the Castle did you see Mr. Thomas Bowes?

A I did not, I called out to them to demand the body of Lady Strathmore:

know some particulars from the people, my information was she was at the Castle

Q What did you think?

A I certainly by seeing the windows barracaded up as they were, thought she was there, the next day I saw Mr Thomas Bowes at the Castle, on the 16th of November I called out, making the same demand I had done the day before, and mentioned that I should be extremely sorry to commit any violence, but I must break open the Castle, and I gave them a quarter of an hour, I pulled out my watch—I waited a quarter of an hour, and the people began to force the way, then a voice called out Mr Farrer I will open the door to let you in with one or two friends, which I supposed to be Mr Thomas Bowes, by no other person being in the hall, I went in, I saw nobody but Mr Thomas Bowes, that leads me to suppose the voice was his, I asked him if Lady Strathmore was there, he hesitated a little, and said she was not, I then asked whether Mr. Bowes was there, he said he was not, I said to Mr. Thomas Bowes, I presume you have seen Lady Strathmore, he said he had not, I told him it was very necessary to search the house, I suspected they were there, and some constables came in and searched the house, and we found they were gone, after which I addressed Mr Bowes immediately, and said, sir, you must certainly know where Mr Bowes and Lady Strathmore are, he said he should not answer any questions upon interrogatories, I then with some warmth mentioned to Mr Bowes I would not be in his skin, knowing, as I conceive he did, where Mr. Bowes and Lady Strathmore were, for the whole county of Durham. I could get no more from him.

Q He knew who you was?

A He certainly did.

Q Lady Strathmore after she was rescued was brought back to your house?

A. I was not in town, she was attended by Mr. Beaumont.

Mr ERSKINE. Q In the first place we are intitled not only to the truth, which I suppose you have told us, but the whole truth, there is another question, you say that upon asking this gentleman Mr Thomas Bowes, where Mr Bowes and Lady Strathmore was, he said he was not bound to answer interrogatories.

A. Yes.

Q. Then you said you would not be in his skin for all the whole county of Durham, knowing, as you conceived he did, where Mr Bowes and Lady Strathmore were, did not he then after that, tell you upon his honor he did not know?

A. I do not recollect that upon my oath

Q. Do you mean to swear that did not pass?

A I really do not believe it did pass, I have no recollection of agreeing to receive his honor as a man, for I suspected his honor and veracity

Q Do you recollect that before Mr Thomas Bowes would allow you to come into the house, he made terms that a poney should not come in?

A. He did.

Mr MINGAY. Is not it to take goods?

A. Yes.

DAVID KIRK, *sworn.*

I am Turnpike-keeper between Brough and Appleby

Q Do you remember seeing Mr Bowes and Lady Strathmore at your Turnpike?

A Yes, on the 17th Day of November last

Q Who were the persons that came to your gate?

A First and foremost there was *Sir Andrew Robinson Bowes*, came to our gate, and called twice gate, gate, I soon went to the door, and opened the door, this gentleman came in, and said what am I to pay you for three horses? Three-pence, says I, he paid me three-pence, and he took a round and looked at the house, so he went out of doors, and made the three horses come through the gate, he took off the Lady in his arms, and fetched her within the door, says he, may this lady warm herself by the fire, says I, very welcome to sit down and warm herself, she was in a man's great coat, with yellow buttons on the sleeve, then he took a shilling and threw

down

down and said 'may be this Lady will drink a dish of tea, and she drank one dish of tea—there was a great deal of snow and sleet that day.

Q. Who was the woman that was with them?

A Her name is Mary Gowland

Q. Was there no more in your house than Mr. Bowes and Lady Strathmore, and Mary Gowland—Did they come from the way of the mountains?

A I thought so.

Q. Did you or your wife make any observations to Mr Bowes about their travelling in that manner at that time of night?

A. The woman wanted, as I fancied, to do something for herself, this Mary Gowland, says I, sir, you have a very bad night to travel in—says he, it is a point of necessity, she has a daughter lying-in, at the point of death, at the point of death, says I, what, at Appleby? Yes, says he, Appleby,—says he again, is there any good inns at Appleby, and I told him of one, I offered to light him; no says he, we want no light, yes says I you do, and two men chucked her on horseback with their hands, and one supported her on, she was behind a man with a shag coat, as I took him, I cannot positively say to that man, I know one Shield that was with him, he was a game-keeper, the Lady was hardly a quarter of an hour in our house—she looked sadly

Mr. FIELDING Q. The gentleman who was with this Lady behaved very civil to the Lady, and wished to accommodate her?

A. I think the gentleman wanted more to accommodate her than she wanted to be accommodated by him—she drank two dishes of tea.

Q. Do you recollect me there?

A You might, I think you are almost like him

Q. Do not you recollect that I was very civil to the Lady—do not you remember my eating some brown bread there?

A. You might.

Q I had not this wig on at that time

A. No, I believe not, the gentleman that was at our house with her had a white cap under his hat.

JAMES ANGIER *sworn.*

I saw Mr. Bowes and some of his people in November at Appleby.

Q Was Lady Strathmore with him?

A. Yes.

Q Who formed the troop?

A. I happened to stand at the door, I keep an Inn at Brough, I saw them get into the chaise, Mr. Bowes came out, and I pulled my hat off, and he said Angier are you here, says he are you come to take me, says he my man tells me you are, but says he if you are, I am very well provided, I have a pistol on each side, says I, if you have sir, I have no business to take you—Lady Strathmore was in the chaise, and seemed very uneasy, I saw her go into the chaise at Appleby—it was very cold weather.

Q Had it been snow?

A There had been a very great deal of snow I saw him before in company with one Mr Peacock and three or four more, they were at my house at Brough, I cannot tell who was with them then.

Q What time of day was it they left Appleby?

A. A quarter past ten.

Q Market day?

A. Yes.

Q The street full of a great number of people?

A There was a great many.

Q. Did Lady Strathmore apply for any assistance?

A I did not hear her speak, she was sitting in the chaise and seemed very uneasy

Q Was she carried into the chaise, or did she walk in as any other traveller?

A. I cannot say.

Mr GARROW. Q Was she moving her hands about as in distress?

A. She was in this way, moving her hands up and down, she appeared very much dejected and distressed.

I ROBERT

ROBERT PEVERILL *sworn.*

MR. LAW. Q What are you?

A I am a grocer at Barnard Castle.

Q Do you recollect your being at Streatlam Castle before or after Mr. Bowes went off?

A I was there after he left the castle and not before.

Q Upon what day was it that you went there?

A On the 24th of November

Q Was Mr. Thomas Bowes there?

A Yes

Q. In any conversation that you had with Mr Thomas Bowes could you learn any thing from him whether he knew any thing of Lady Strathmore being carried from the castle?

A. I enquired if my Lady and Mr. Bowes were there, and I was told by Mr. Thomas Bowes they were not.

Q When was this?

A The 24th

Q That cannot be?

A It was on the Monday I imagined the Tipstaff had been there, but I saw nothing off it—the castle was barred up.

Q Did Mr Thomas Bowes tell you why the castle was barred up?

A No, he did not

Q Who put you into the castle?

A. I went to see my Lady and Mr. Bowes.

Q Who let you in?

A. Mr. Thomas Bowes—he locked me in, I never did learn the cause of it from him, I did not know the cause till afterwards.

Q. Did you recollect attempting to go out at any time?

A I was glad to get out, Mr. Bowes said he desired I would not, for if I did attempt to go out other people would come in.

Q. What else did he say, did not he say if you open the door you would ruin all?

A I do not know

Q Did not you see Peter Orme pick up the papers and carry them to Mr. Thomas Bowes?

A I saw the papers lying all of them, I was there, I never looked at them nor touched them

Q Were they carried to Mr. Thomas Bowes?

A I believe they were

Q What did he say?

A. He said it must be sent back again and not to be looked at.

Q Do you know what the papers were?

A I really do not

MR ERSKINE. Q Did not Mr. Thomas Bowes carry you to the window of the castle at the time you wanted to get out, and shew you through the window of the castle the numbers of people that were there?

A I dare not go out, the people threatned on the outside, I scarce durst to have ventured out

Q Did not he tell you in the clearest manner, that his reason for not letting you out was for fear of letting the people in?

A Undoubtedly, there were fires arround us, I heard guns and fire arms.

Q Was not that an alarming situation for the people that were within the castle?

A. Most certainly

MR MINGAY. Q When you first went in, was there any body to alarm?

A No, I tried at two doors and could not get in

MR ERSKINE. Q Did not Mr. Thomas Bowes tell you that there were processes against Mr. Robinson Bowes?

A Yes.

ANN

ANN HARRISON *sworn*

I live at Branton—On the 18th of November about one, I saw Mr. Bowes, but he called himself a doctor.

Q Who did the doctor bring with him?

A. There was nobody in the coach with him, he applied to me for a horse to carry a woman to Copelandbeck, I let him have one, he said he had been in a chaise and the chaise had broke down, and he wanted a horse to carry a woman to Copelandbeck, I went with him to Copelandbeck

ABRAHAM DUNN *sworn.*

I was sent after Mr Bowes, by Mrs Liddell.

Q. Did you see Mr Bourn, the steward?

A. Yes—I saw him three miles off Darlington.

Q. What alarm did he give to these persons?

A I did not hear him

Q. What did he say?

A I did not hear him say any thing—he followed me—I was in pursuit of Mr. Bowes, with other people—he followed me into Darlington—I did not see much more of him—he turned back again and went to meet Mr Bowes—I saw him take his horse and go back.

Q Do you know whether he met Mr Bowes?

A. I cannot tell.

Mr. CHAMBRE. Q Did you see Lady Strathmore?

A Yes.

Q Did you hear her speak to anybody?

A. No—I never heard her say any thing till she was rescued.

ROBERT THORNTON *sworn*

Q Was you present at the time Bourn came up?

A No—I do not know Bourn.

CHRISTOPHER SMITH *sworn.*

I am constable of the parish of Neasham—I came up with Mr Bowes and Lady Strathmore, he had a pair of loaded pistols, one in his hand and the other in his belt, on his left side—he asked me what I wanted, and I told him the country was alarmed about him, and we came to take him, he said he would blow the first man's brains out that offered to touch him—I told him if he would surrender I would not hurt him—he presented his pistol to the whole company several times—Lady Strathmore seemed to jump off the horse

Q Who took hold of her?

A. William Stubbs—Gabriel Thornton was at a small distance.

Q What became of Mr Bowes then?

A I knocked him off his horse—Thornton came up, and we carried him to the alehouse, and sent for a surgeon to look at his wounds

Q. Did he surrender?

A There was no occasion for a surrender when he was knocked off his horse, I think.

MR. BEAUMONT, Surgeon, *sworn.*

I saw Lady Strathmore the following morning after she was rescued—she was in a very deplorable state indeed!

Q State to my Lord, her Ladyship's condition.

A From the severity of the weather and the ill treatment she had suffered, I thought her life in great danger—she was coming down to the Court, but was not able to come
down

down stairs by herself—she was quite a feeble woman—she continued in that state, I dare say, very near a month, and she was full a month before she could stand.

Q. Did you examine her legs?

A. I did—her feet particularly—her ancles were much contracted and difcoloured, which evidently were the effect of the weather, seemingly as if they had been numbed.

Mr. ERSKINE. Do not you know that she was frequently lame before and in that situation?

A. Never.

Mr. MINGAY. Q. Would she have been in that situation before, unless she had been numbed by cold weather?

A. I look upon it entirely owing to the weather.

Mr. ERSKINE.

May it pleafe your Lordship: Gentlemen of the Jury; No man can poffibly lament more than I do, that fuch a connection as fubfifts, or rather ought to fubfift between the gentleman who fits by me, and the profecutrix of this indictment, fhould be productive of fuch confequences, that the hufband and wife, which is moft undoubtedly inftituted by fociety to be the folace of human life, and for the production and the protection of pofterity, from which fo many real enjoyments ought to arife, and in which the public is fo very much interefted in the prefervation of, fhould be in this manner turned into bitternefs and gall, that, on the one hand, the wife fhould appear againft the hufband, as the profecutrix of an indictment for a confpiracy, and, on the other hand, that the hufband fhould recriminate againft the wife, by an indictment for perjury. Gentlemen, a man muft be loft, not only to all Chriftian, but, I fhould apprehend, to all human feelings, who does not feel infinitely hurt at every thing that has been ftated this day, and if you fat there to try what were the motives of Mr Bowes for carrying off this lady, which you do on fome counts of this indictment, if you fat there to try the meafure of thefe enormities, I fhould be bound to confume a great deal more of my Lord's time and your's to call a number of witneffes—I fhould detain you all the night, and perhaps the next day, in contradicting many of thofe acts of turpitude, and in fhewing that many of them are the fabrications of Lady Strathmore, who brings this information before you, but, as my learned friend, kindly to me, was pleafed, by way of anticipation, to make a defence for me, yet I fhould ill deferve that, or any other compliment, if I did not adopt, what I conceive to be the firft of all abilities in a counfel, namely, that which I hinted to my Lord, decency and difcretion. There are cafes where eloquence, if it were poffeffed, as furely it is not by me, weighs nothing but to difguft. Is it poffible to fuppofe men can be difcourfed out of their reafon? or, if you could, that all the authority of the Court that is to follow me, is likewife to be taken away, and my Lord alfo is to be difcourfed out of the oath he has taken to the public, and his knowledge of the law, whatever therefore goes only as a mitigation of any circumftance which may be brought home to Mr. Bowes, is not the fubject of inveftigation to-day, therefore with refpect to all thefe acts of cruelty which may be fuppofed to exift, they are hereafter to be inveftigated, where they are the jet of the profecution, where the falfhood is the fubject of an indictment for perjury, and where, if a jury find it to be falfe, Mr Bowes may come to obtain from the Court that mitigating fentence which will arife from many of thefe facts on which this caufe is founded, being found to be falfe. Gentlemen, this profecution is inftituted by Lady Strathmore, and moft unqueftionably has this foundation in law, that the wife has a right to the protection of the law to keep herfelf from violence, even againft the hufband, and, although he may have a right of poffeffion of her perfon, he can neither feize or detain that perfon by force, and therefore this is a profecution that has for its object the fecurity of an individual, who is to be protected by rules that neceffarily involve a much greater degree of caution than the fecurity of all the individuals in the world, and, confequently, the fafety of the public, becaufe before a jury are to convict men of any crime, however they may feel hurt, however they may deteft the conduct, yet when they come to confider the cafe, they will do it in a grave and difpaffionate manner, they will not fuffer their imaginations to be heated, and to run away with them, and, therefore, notwithftanding all the prejudice that has been attempted to be excited, I have no doubt but you will give as good a verdict as if we had

been

been calmly confidering the cafe. Gentlemen, let us fee the different charges, what they are—I have obferved it is natural enough for men to be agitated at acts of cruelty — but you have not yet had this cafe ftated with any accuracy, becaufe it is particularly material to all the parties, and particularly to two of them, how much of this charge you fhall find to be true. There are five different charges in the information, and my Lord will tell you they they are all as diftinct and independent, as if drawn on feparate parchments. The firft charge is, that Lady Strathmore had commenced a fuit againft Mr Bowes in the Spiritual Court for a feparation and divorce, that all the defendants, well knowing the premifes, did confpire together to ftop the profecution of that fuit, and in purfuance of that confpiracy, made an affault on her upon the 10th of November, carried her away, imprifoned her for ten days, expofed her to the feverity of the weather, againft the peace. This is the firft count of the information, the fecond and third charge the fame things, and my Lord will tell you, that even if on thefe three counts in the information, you fhould be perfectly fatisfied that thefe defendants all of them confpired to imprifon Lady Strathmore upon the fuggeftion of Mr Bowes, that he defired to have her perfon in his poffeffion, but not knowing that the object of that wifh on the part of Mr Bowes was the ftopping this fuit, whatever acts of cruelty they committed, whatever affault and violence was committed to whatever inclemency of the weather fhe was expofed—but it is not neceffary for me in this ftage of the bufinefs to contravert—I fay, my Lord will bear me out in afferting, that upon thefe three counts in the information, all the defendants not having the knowledge of that object on the part of Mr. Bowes, it cannot be brought home to them by reafonable evidence, and they cannot be convicted on thefe counts in the information, which charges a confpiracy for that purpofe. There is a difference between what lawyers call inducement, and the fubftance of the charge, the fubftance of the charge is, that they confpired together, not to imprifon Lady Strathmore, for I am willing to admit that there is fuch ftrong evidence againft fome of the defendants for imprifoning her, that it I was to think I could by mere words deftroy the effect of what has been proved, to attempt to acquit all the defendants of all the charges, as men of fenfe you muft laugh at me. Let us obferve then what evidence there is before you that any of the defendants, except a perfon of the name of Bickley, confpired with Mr Bowes, or confpired amongft one another, to ftop this fuit in the Commons, inftituted by Lady Strathmore againft her hufband. Now it may be afked, fince there are two charges of which you will be obliged, perhaps, to find many of the defendants guilty—Why am I fo eager to acquit them of this? I faid before, if you had authority to fay what Mr. Bowes, or any other of the defendants fhould fuffer for thefe acts, I muft then go into all the evidence, in order by mitigation to obtain from you a light fentence, but as you can only by your verdict fay guilty or not guilty, and guilty of this charge, which perhaps may be confiftant with not guilty in another charge, and as it is the duty of the Court to fay what punifhment they fhall have, it becomes extremely material to the juftice of the cafe, and the folemn duty impofed on you to fay where you nad there is evidence to convict, and where there is not. Men of honorable feelings when circumftances are laid before them fuch as thefe, it is no wonder that the human mind fhould revolt againft every thing that feeks to cover and protect fuch people as are charged, and I cannot but feel myfelf very much obliged to you to liften to me for perfons, for whom you certainly have no great inclination, but, however, it may be a pleafant thing to men who feel as you ought to do on fuch fubjects, to inflict punifhment and to bring the offenders to juftice, yet you will remember that people have a right to be heard in their defence, before that juftice ought to pafs, for if men have not opportunities of applying to the Judges and Jury of their country, confpiracies would be very rife indeed, and no man could fay that health and liberty, or his property in this free country, were in fafety. I am now fpeaking of all the defendants, except a perfon of the name of Bickley, if my Lord does not confirm what I fay— if he fays the law as I ftate it to you is not correctly ftated, difcharge from your mind what I fay, and attend to him, but if the charge in the three firft counts is one firft whether you are fatisfied that thefe defendants did confpire to ftop the procefs of the law, it will be the better courfe to fay at once that I have no evidence by which I can protect Mr Peacock, Mr Prevot, Mr Chapman, Mr Pigg, and Mr. Bickley, and the defendant, Mr Andrew Robinfon Bowes, from the 5th count in the indictment— I have none—I am prepared with a great deal of evidence to mitigate the confpiracy of

K

whidi

which they have undoubtedly been guilty against the law, but for the reason I have mentioned, I do not think it discreet to produce it, there are many reasons that induced Mr Bowes, most undoubtedly, to have possession of his wife—very different reasons from those assigned in the first count of this indictment, and it is a melancholy consideration, that that which would operate as a man's best defence, would operate also to his shame and disgrace—so near is the connection in which they stand, that a man cannot disgrace the prosecutrix without disgracing himself, the nature of the connection is, that all our honour, their happiness—I might say, their very being are so connected, that when a man endeavours to criminate his wife, he must come into a share of it himself. if a wife squanders the property of her husband, or runs into debt, or lives in improper company there can be no sort of doubt that he may take his wife into his possession, provided she is not either separated by consent, or by the act of law, either separated by the process of the Court, or by her own act, but he cannot do it by circumstances of force—he cannot do it by circumstances of terror to the King's subjects.

COURT If you mean to make it your defence that he took her for the purpose of avoiding idle expences, you might ask the question you waved before

Mr ERSKINE If Mr Bowes, had taken his wife into his possession, in a manner which would have rendered that taking legal, from those motives, I should then have desired to have called those witnesses because if I had proved that which I expected to prove, and which I undoubtedly could prove, I should have asked permission to do it I conceived my Lord rejected my application on this ground, that let the motive be however pure however honourable, however correct, however perhaps laudable and humane, for it may be highly humane to take a woman out of the hands of persons that are conspiring to ruin her by amusing her with lies of fortune-tellers, in order to widen the breach with the husband, and to prevent that union which is much to the honor of all persons, if Mr Bowes had taken his wife into his possession peaceably, he would have been protected by the law, but whatever may be his motive, discretion is the best ability, it is impossible that I can defend him against that illegal act for taking his wife into his own possession, and as you can have only to pronounce the verdict of guilty on that fifth count, it will be therefore for me where I am able, to shew the motives, the honorable, the just and pure motives that induced Mr Bowes to transgress the laws, and it will be for the court to say, what is the punishment that a man ought to receive who transgresses the law from one motive or another I therefore have so conducted myself, and I hope when I conduct myself in this manner, instead of endeavouring to impose on your understandings, when I declare I cannot attempt to defend any of the defendants, except Mr Bourne and Mr Thomas Bowes who stands there, from the charge in the fifth count, I hope I shall be honored with your attention, when I observe I shall not offer a sentence to day however weak, I shall offer none that will shock your understandings, or your reason, or that I think my Lord will be disposed to animadvert upon, which he would do, if not well founded when adduced by counsel at the bar. I apprehend, that on those other counts, which do not charge a conspiracy only, but charge one to stop the proceedings she had instituted in the commons, and that in pursuance of that conspiracy to stop that suit in the commons, they seized her violently and took her that it will be necessary some how, to connect them with the knowledge of that suit being instituted, for it is repugnant to common sense, to say I conspire to stop a suit with the existence of which I am not acquainted, or that I conspire with him, unless it was known to me that Mr Bowes had that object Now Orme is the first witness in this cause, and there was as much reason to suppose Mr. Bowes should put as much trust in him, as in Lucas or any of the others that witness being examined, furnishes a lesson of caution, particularly where gentlemen in your situation are to decide on the liberties of the people, for you would be obliged to go blindfold in the conviction of Orme, supposing him to be convicted of that of which he says he was not guilty, and it furnishes me with this observation, that Orme is not at all connected with the knowledge that these people had. if my learned friend could have got these people together, and could shew that he ever mentioned his object in taking her was to stop the suit, the men to whom that act is brought home, are conspirators under the three first counts in the indictment I then admit for the same reason, (still laying in my claim when you find that I distinguish between causes that are tenable and those that are not) I admit Bickley is so fixed, for you find he said it was to stop this

prosecution,

profecution, there is a knowledge in Bickley, it may be faid, it may be left to you what is the decifion, what you think you ought to find, it may be faid, that fince Bickley knew this he muft know it from Mr. Bowes: that Mr Bowes muft have communicated it to Bickley, that, that was his object, or he could not communicate it to Orme, it may be faid you will infer it, you will prefume it. Gentlemen, it is contrary to the genius of the law of this country, fuch large and fuch weak prefumptions as thefe, wherever a man can have any diftinct and direct evidence againft him, it is fit he fhould fuffer the penalties of the law, and thefe men muft fuffer thefe penalties in that count where they ought to be convicted, and I do not know, whether it will make much difference, between that and their being convicted on the whole indictment. but it is my duty to ftate what I conceive to be the cafe, which is, that it would be extremely dangerous, if a defire in a jury to bring people to punifhment, which defire has for its object, the fecurity of an individual, fhould carry them farther then the evidence will warrant, and fhould lead them to prefume any thing that is not fupported by proof, for in that cafe how can a man be fafe in his life, liberty, property or reputation how indeed, but in the ftrict manner of the adminiftration of the laws, in which nothing is to be prefumed and taken for granted, but what you fee certain as you fee my hand before me I therefore repeat that there is not a tittle of evidence out of the twenty-five or twenty fix perfons that have been examined, there is not directly nor indirectly, any thing that fixes on any one of thefe defendants a knowledge of the fuit being in exiftence, or that if it was, that he meant by this means to ftop it if you are of that opinion, moft unqueftionably you will fay fo by your verdict, and you will find that all the defendants except Bourn and Thomas Bowes, did confpire to imprifon Lady Strathmore, but that they did not confpire to ftop that fuit in the commons Gentlemen, I now come to that which I conceive to be a matter where I fhall have no prejudices to ftruggle againft, I am now to addrefs you on the part of Mr Thomas Bowes, who ftands by my learned friend Mr Lee, and I fhall take the liberty prefently of afking Mr Lee what character he bears, whether he is not a man of fair and honeft reputation, becaufe certainly where there is any doubt, or as here where there is very little doubt or no doubt, an anfwer to fuch a queftion, fuch as Mr Lee will give, will have great effect, and will be of very great confequence indeed, for becaufe a gentleman, for reafons beft known to himfelf, we will fuppofe improper ones, choofes to lay hold of his wife by violence, and carry her down to his houfe at the diftance of two hundred miles, if it was to involve every fervant, or every attorney employed, what would be the confequence? Mr Thomas Bowes was engaged in fuits for Mr Robinfon Bowes, and that accounts for the correfpondence, without prefuming that correfpondence had for its object the illegal conduct of the others. you are told that Mr Thomas Bowes was employed as attorney for Mr Bowes, with refpect to the letters that are carried, they were carried by a man of the name of Stockel, who tells you that he brought money, but the fubject of this letter is totally unknown, the firft witnefs that is called to you on this fubject is Orme, who told you that when the chaife ftopped at the door my Lady was handed out, and another witnefs faid, fhe defired to have it made public, that fhe did not give her confent, but was brought there by force, there is no proof of any fort or kind, which can leave you to fancy that Mr Thomas Bowes knew that my Lady was under any reftraint, there is nothing before you either directly or indirectly, from whence the knowledge can be imputed to Mr Thomas Bowes, that he brought her away without her confent, or if he did, that fhe was not then perfectly reconciled Orme fays they faw her no more, whether Mr Thomas Bowes faw her, or what fhe communicated to him, whether fhe related to him any part of the ill treatment, does not appear but the queftion is not whether or no Mr Bowes connived at the imprifonment of this Lady in the county of Durham, not whether he aided and affifted Mr Bowes, but whether he confpired with the others, either for the purpofe of ftopping this fuit in the commons, or whether he confpired previous to the 10th of November, previous to that day, the way it is ftated is this, Mr Bowes had been in London fome time before, meditating moft undoubtedly to get poffeffion of this Lady, finding he was difcovered, and anxious not to appear to be concerned in it, he goes back to his Caftle in the north, and there he fends Bourne to Hobfon, defiring him to entruft him with this fecret that he is much deranged in his affairs, that he has fell from his horfe, Hobfon is to be fent for, Hobfon who is impofed on by Bowes, who believes he is in that

fituation,

situation, he bleeds him and carries on the farce, this is another lesson of caution; suppose Hobson had been a defendant here, supposing it had been proved that he had been bleeding a man that had no fall, that he was going on a farce for ten days—Good God! gentlemen, if Hobson had been a defendant, so as not to have an opportunity of speaking for himself, is not that the situation of Mr Thomas Bowes? Why you would have said, has not this man practised a fraud?— Has not he been entrusted by Bowes? Has not he contrived the very scheme for putting that illegal act into execution? Has not he acted a part in the play, which was only the prologue to what followed? But from the circumstances of this gentleman not being put into that situation, of his being made a witness instead of being made a defendant, he has the opportunity of stating the whole fact, and the most important evidence he gives for Mr Thomas Bowes, you observe the defendant never communicated his real purpose to Mr Thomas Hobson for his appearing ill, but only that his affairs were deranged, he is asked upon cross-examination, and Mr Bowes instructed me to put it, I hope I am not irregular in putting this, for as there is no interposition of a grand jury, in the information he has the opportunity of exculpating himself, and my friends know on his solemn oath Mr Thomas Bowes has denied all knowledge of the matter: the Court then never foresaw that he was to be prosecuted for a crime in the county of Middlesex, he may be prosecuted by another sort of prosecution, and in my Lord's hearing I say, if you should believe he did connive at the imprisonment of Lady Strathmore in Durham, if you believe he did connive at the violence which is not warranted, yet unless you have evidence to your satisfaction that he knew previous to coming to the Castle, that Mr Bowes was about to imprison her, then he is not guilty on this information, and I profess when the Court made the rule absolute I thought it was this, by information of imprisonment in that county, but you must be convinced of this, no man can tell where such a thing would reach, and in actually seeking to do justice, and preserve the peace, you would destroy all peace; the question now is whether you can upon your oaths say as a jury, that you are convinced upon evidence, not what you imagine, not what is probable, not what is possible, but whether you are convinced that Mr Thomas Bowes, antecedently to the time of his going back to his home, knew he was going back for the purpose of bringing Lady Strathmore up, that he conspired with him for that purpose, if he is not guilty of that, however he might in such an instance be amenable, he is to day guiltless, he is not chargeable with any of these crimes that are made the subject of this information. Hobson is asked whether he has any reason to believe that Thomas Bowes knew he was sick, he says he had no reason to think that he knew his sickness was a sham, on the contrary, that he had messages from others who did not wish to let him into the light; you are to presume not merely without evidence, but in violation of the only evidence that has been adduced to criminate, and what other evidence is there? for it seems to me if Mr Bowes would not trust him with this sham sickness, he certainly would not trust him with the other business, why he would have been the first man to know this circumstance, by which alone it could have been carried on, and yet you observe if Orme and Hobson had stood in the situation of Bowes, they would have been equally charged, you see that there were other processes out against Mr. Bowes, he expected to have his goods attached, that he made it one of the terms of admitting Mr Farrer into the Castle, that he would not permit the execution of these ponies, so that you observe he was not left as the steward of Mr. Bowes, but as his attorney, and there is no proof before you that Mr. Bowes then offered her any violence, he saw them go away, and he has solemnly sworn, he had every reason to believe that they went in perfect affection together, when Ridgway came, he tells you the Castle was surrounded by a variety of country people, that the people threatened to rush in, for what purpose? why to heap vengeance on every body within the walls, he says it was an alarming situation—Ridgway says, that he asked him what was become of Mr. Bowes and Lady Strathmore, to which he said I cannot hold any conversation with you, but Ridgway says, he shut the window and went into the Castle before he read the Habeas Corpus, and therefore cannot tell whether he heard that proclamation or not, if we were examining whether Thomas Bowes has been guilty of any of these counts, then you might say according to your judgement on the case, but that question you are not trying, the question is, whether before the 10th of November, before this lady was seized, he did assist Mr Bowes, who is charged with it: I submit in point of law that it would be absolutely necessary to prove some overt act, against Mr Thomas Bowes, as a conspirator, in the county of Middlesex, if the conspiracy was carried into effect by any thing to be done in another county, he must be tried in that county, this is certainly the law, there can be no accessary after the fact in trespass, all are equally guilty both in treason and trespass, therefore as it is not certain that Mr Bowes knew of any intention in Mr Robinson Bowes to carry off his wife, I shall do no injury to my clients if I were to admit that he either knew it, or had a suspicion of it, if he has been guilty of any act at all, it is in not raising the country, and not assisting in the liberation of Lady Strathmore, suppose then he is guilty of an act against the law in the county of Durham, suppose he is guilty of continuing the imprisonment, and knew of the imprisonment, yet there is no sort of proof which fixes him with any knowledge of the intention of Mr Robinson Bowes to carry back his wife, and there is but one day charged in this indictment. Gentlemen, with respect to Mr Bourn, many of the observations apply to him, he is the steward of this gentleman, it would be very severe and very harsh if whatever reason you may have to punish Mr Bowes, you are to involve every man who is at all connected with Mr Bowes in that original trespass committed by him, without any proof before you, now what proof is there before you that Bourn knew that Mr Bowes was going back again to the South—he knew there was no real fall—he knew it was a sham—he knew Bowes was not hurt, and immediately a man is apt to say, does not this look very suspicious, that Bourn should know this? Why Hobson is in the same situation, and he did not know it—Orme did not know it—that is the difference between suspicion and proof, and it would give one pain to observe on evidence, where a man cannot see his way. It does not at all appear that Bourn knew from Mr Bowes, what was his purpose for falling, I offered to produce every letter—we had them all in Court ready to produce—they have never been called for, the production of a letter from one defendant to another can be no evidence for either, because they must be all clear, but it proves that in the minds of the conductors of this prosecution, they thought there was no use in these letters, because they might have asked for them, and which would have answered every end they could possibly have in the producing them, if the rules of evidence warranted such production. Gentlemen, Lady Strathmore is before said by Mr Rippon to have come home in Mr Bowes's great coat, and Thomas Wade says, that as Lady Strathmore was getting out, she said she was brought there by force, and that he had a conversation with Bourn about the cause of her calling out, who asked him if he had not like to have overturned the carriage. Gentlemen, from the time she came out of the Castle into the coach, no witness saw her, how far she was soothed you cannot say, it is not true that she made any complaint to Bourn—that she made any complaint to T. Bowes, or to any one person at Streatlam Castle, that would at least have shewn that they had not acted a proper part, but you are left wholly in the dark as to that, for there is not one instance, there is not any one witness that has come and sworn that he heard her complain, and there has not been a witness called, that I recollect, who has proved to you that Lady Strathmore ever spoke to Mr. Thomas Bowes or to Bourn stating her situation, asking assistance, and complaining of it afterwards, it appears that Bourn speaks to different persons in the Castle, and says he was very much surprised that Mr Bowes was gone to London—but so he was, he had no reason to think so. Gentlemen, I believe I may say without hazarding any contradiction, even in your minds, when I am stating the proposition, that there is not any one fact or circumstance, much less in the combination, to lead to a certain conclusion that either Mr. Bourn, or particularly Mr. Thomas Bowes, knew that he had the intention of carrying away Lady Strathmore, or that they aided or assisted him in that intention, if you are of that opinion, then unquestionably you will acquit them on this record, because you never can say that men are guilty of conspiring to do an act, when you cannot say that there is any one circumstance of their guilt. Gentlemen, I am sure I need not remind you of the great importance in every cause of this sort, to distinguish between the innocent and the guilty, where there has been reasonable evidence of guilt, I hope I have not attempted by observation to do away proof, but that I have confined myself to the proper province of a council, to distinguish the different charges one from another—to distinguish the different charges, I imagine, that Robinson Bowes and the other defendants, all but Bourn and Thomas Bowes, are most undoubtedly subject to be convicted on the fifth count of this information;

L   and

and if you think that they knew of the purpose for which she was carried off, most undoubtedly under the three first counts, but that there is no evidence against Bourn and Bowes, and I humbly submit that there is not even evidence to go to a Jury against them, in as much as if there had been a conspiracy to carry off this Lady on the 10th of November, that that would be an overt act of that conspiracy in the county of Durham, which must be the subject of an information, or an indictment in that county. If my Lord should be of that opinion, then there will be nothing to be left to you at all on the subject of these two gentlemen, if on the other hand he should not be of that opinion, then you will think whether you can say with firmness, that these gentlemen, or either of them, and particularly the last of them that stands near me, can be at all affected with having taken any active part in seizing this Lady, which is the only charge. Gentlemen, I shall call only my learned and worthy friend Mr Lee, merely to answer that single question, to say, whether Mr Thomas Bowes is, or is not, a man of character, because it requires, and ought to require much more evidence to convict a man who has a fair and honest reputation in the world, and if you consider the situation in which this gentleman stands, that it is almost ruin to him and his family, as an attorney, intrusted with other people's affairs, when you consider the consequence of your verdict, you will certainly examine the evidence with great correctness, if you have reason to find him guilty, no consequence that can arise to himself, or any character can avail, but if there is nothing but surmise and possibility, for I will not use the word probability, in that case you will acquit him, and Gentlemen, the question is, Whether there is sufficient proof to convict a man of that crime in his situation?

Mr. LEE *offered to be sworn.*

Mr MINGAY I consent to it as if upon oath

Mr LEE. I have known Mr. Thomas Bowes many years, I believe ever since the time I have gone the Northern circuit, or at least ever since I have gone to reside in the county of Durham, I have known him in business pretty frequently—known a good deal of his reputation, and I never heard any thing against him, I think, in my life—I do not think I have known a practiser of fairer character than he has borne; and from that time, I say nothing relative to this matter, about which, indeed, I know nothing but from rumor, but I never did know a man of his profession, bear a fairer or more honourable character in my life

C O U R T.

GENTLEMEN of the JURY.

This is an information against the several defendants, who are nine in number, and they stand charged—first, with conspiring to take and imprison Lady Strathmore, in order to oblige her to drop a prosecution which was then depending in the Ecclesiastical Court, by which she sought to obtain a divorce against Mr Bowes her husband There is another charge for a conspiracy to imprison her, and another for assaulting and imprisoning her, without stating any conspiracy With respect to the first seven defendants, Andrew Robinson Bowes, Edward Lucas, Francis Peacock, Mark Prevot, Charles Chapman, William Pigg, and John Bickley, it has been proved that these seven were all acting upon the spot in the county of Middlesex, and in a case of this length, where the facts of the case have been proved over and over again by different witnesses, it does not seem to me, that I should render any essential service to you by repeating all the evidence to you over again, the substance of it is, that in the year 1785, the suit in the Ecclesiastical Court for a divorce was commenced, that that suit was depending on the 10th of November, 1786, at the time this Lady was taken away in the manner you have heard, it has been proved that previous to that time, the defendant Bowes, passing under feigned names, and for what reason has not been assigned, in company with others of the defendants, who likewise went under borrowed names, had been watching in different parts, in order to surprise this Lady, and that at last they got possession of her by means that must shock every man in this country, who has the smallest regard for his personal liberty or safety Here is a charge trumped up, for so I may call it, in as much as no evidence has been given, under which a

warrant

warrant is got from a magistrate to apprehend her two servants that attended her, her coachman and footman, that is carried on by a man, who at the time filled the office of a constable—a peace officer is proved to have been one of the most active in carrying this plan into execution, they take her by force, and carry her through the publick streets of London as far as Highgate, some of them giving out that she is to go before Lord Mansfield at Caen Wood, at Highgate she is met by Mr. Bowes, and from thence they carry her two hundred and forty miles in the space of thirty hours, or thereabouts, she repeatedly crying murder, and intreating assistance and none could be obtained, and she is carried to Streatlam Castle by these men, not long to remain there, because she is carried in the dead of the night from thence in a very cold and inclement season, over mountains to different houses, at which they thought it necessary to secrete themselves, and so she is carried about from place to place, till she is rescued by the people of the country. This is the general outline of the business, and the first question for your consideration will be, what was the end and object of all this conduct in Mr. Bowes? It is said on the part of the prosecution, it was for the purpose of getting rid of that suit which was depending in the Ecclesiastical Court. No other reason whatever has been suggested on the part of the defendants, it has been proved that this suit was then going on, and had been pretty far advanced, and one of the witnesses tells you, all these defendants have acted in the design of taking her and putting her into the possession of that man, against whom that suit was brought. One of the defendants, Bickley, after he had attended some time part of the way, and had got as far as Barnet, assigns as the reason, that Mr. Bowes had some law-suit depending, and it was necessary to have Lady Strathmore when the cause came on, and he had been employed by Bowes three weeks, at two guineas a week, this man therefore surely knows of the cause—How could he know it?—Could he know it but by Mr. Bowes? You find it proved that all the other five defendants are with Mr. Bowes, and lodged under feigned names, that they dodged her from time to time, and when on the North road this is the reason assigned by him. The next evidence is what passed at St. Iron, there I think there were five of the defendants, also Mr. Bowes was alone with her in the room when he wanted to make her sign a paper, he called for pen, ink, and paper, wrote some lines, and when the waiter went in again, Mr. Bowes was standing by her, and he heard Lady Strathmore say, I will not sign it for you nor any body, you see again by Mr. Bowes's conduct what is the object he had in view, there are five other defendants that are then with him, they forced her into the carriage, it is true they are not in the room when this passes, but the question is, whether they who accompanied him in this business, did not know the view in the proceeding which Mr. Bowes had, and which Bickley avowed he had, if they all knew it, then there cannot be a doubt but these seven defendants must be convicted. The Council for the defendants has very ably endeavoured to distinguish between the cases of the several defendants, and pointed out to you that there is no express evidence of this design being known to any body but Bowes and Bickley, it is my duty to tell you, that in point of law you cannot convict those two defendants alone of this conspiracy, conspiracy necessarily implies that three or more persons have been engaged in it, and if on the whole of the evidence, you should be of opinion that there is no guilt to be imputed to any of the defendants as far as the conspiracy goes, you must necessarily acquit them all, but upon this subject it will be material to consider a little what the law is as to conspiracies in general, if several persons engage in a conspiracy to do an illegal act, and each man takes his part, though the full end, design, and secret be not known to all but one, yet if all will boldly engage under the banner of that man who is the principal, if they are determined to go all lengths he may require to effect his purpose, and that purpose be effected, all will be answerable to the full extent of the crime, so it is in the case of more serious offences, with which our law books are filled, if a number of persons will engage in an illegal act, and one of them who is the great mover of the business has some secret design in his mind to commit a murder, if in pursuance of that act he kills a person totally unknown to all the rest, yet if it be done in pursuance of that illegal combination, all of them are clearly guilty of murder. Upon these observations it will be for you to say, whether on the evidence you have heard, you are of opinion or not, that the seven first defendants are all proved to be conspiring with Mr. Bowes, and acting with him in that design, for the purpose of prevailing on Lady Strathmore to sign this paper, if so, the seven defendants are guilty. Then the question will be, whether they all concurred in the act of imprisoning her in the manner stated by the third and fourth courts. With respect to the other two defendants,

Bou.

Bourn and Thomas Bowes, their cases certainly stand in a different light; therefore I will state to you separately and distinctly, what is the evidence that affects either the one or the other, and I will begin with Bourn   Thomas Wade is the first witness that speaks of Bourn, he was the postillion at Greta Bridge, he drove Mr Bowes and Lady Strathmore—she cried out several times, and said she was brought there by force, and desired it might be made publick, says he, I saw Bourn there, he said he supposed I had like to have overturned the carriage, which made Lady Strathmore cry out so—I told him that was impossible, because she never cried out till she was out of the carriage—he asked what she called out for, and he said it was likely he should know as well as him—Does not this conversation import that he knew what she said—that he had heard her cry out, or else he could never charge the postillion?—there was no danger—there was no probability of her being over-turned, and the witness remarked to him at the time, that she did not cry out till she was out of the carriage, the question therefore is, whether on this evidence you do not see Bourn practising this artifice in order to throw a false colour, and mislead Wade   Thomas Colpits says, this was before Bowes came to London, on the 25th of October, I was at Barnard Castle and observed Mr Robinson Bowes, Bourn, and Prevot mount their horses, and proceed towards Streatlam, when they had gone a sufficient time to get to Streatlam, Bourn returned in a violent hurry to call Hobson the surgeon, the surgeon went off, and Bourne gave out at the post-house, that Mr Bowes had received a very bad accident on the road, that his horse had fallen, and that he had pitched over him two or three times—Hobson is understood to bleed him—Bourn came up with a post-chaise—Bourn and Prevot returned and counted his money, and they put Bowes into the chaise, and Bourn and Hobson returned to the Castle.—Here then you see that Bourn is acting on some design that has not been explained, that there is some artifice going on between Mr Bowes and the defendant Bourn, so early as the 25th of October   The next witness, Robert Hobson, tells you he was sent for—Bourn was the man that came to him—then Bowes asked him if he could keep a secret, and then he told him of this intended plan to fall off his horse, and Bowes gave him a letter to copy for Mr. Lee, and then he tells you on the 5th or 6th of November, Bourn told him that Bowes was in London, and that he had received a letter, and that he wished to have it said that Mr. Bowes went off the night before by express, the question is, What can this conduct be attributed to, unless he was in the secret of Bowes's going to London on his business there?

On the 25th of October, a fortnight before this Lady is taken, you find him acting his part with Bowes, which is proved to be a mere fiction, Bowes goes to London, then he wants to have a false date given to the time of going to London—why should he wish that? he desires it may be said he went off by express. The next witness that speaks of Bourn is Abraham Dunn—says he, I went in pursuit of Mr. Bowes, I saw Bourn three miles from Darlington, he followed me to Darlington, then he went back to meet Bowes—this is the whole of the evidence against Bourn   With respect to him, you see he is acting a very strange part, at least with Bowes, long before this Lady is taken, his conduct is totally unaccounted for or unexplained—he lives in Mr. Bowes's house, he is so far in his secret, as appears by the evidence, that he is the man entrusted with the letter when he arrives in London, and he is the person to propagate the falsehood, as to the time when he sat out, besides that, you hear from different witnesses, the conduct Bourn was guilty of, after Lady Strathmore was brought to Streatlam Castle, now with respect to this defendant, and likewise the defendant Thomas Bowes, you have been told at the bar, that it is necessary in point of law, that some overt act must be proved against them in Middlesex, in my opinion, the true rule is this, if these defendants Bourn and Bowes were privy and assenting to the design, before Lady Strathmore was taken away—if they are proved to have advised or concurred in it, they are all equally guilty with those who acted on the spot, and in the case of a conspiracy, one can only pick up the acts and knowledge of the different parties, from what it appears they have done in the different stages of the business, even independant of that evidence which I have stated to you against Bourn. On the 25th of October, prior to the time Lady Strathmore was taken, there is that evidence which I am bound to submit to your consideration, for though it should be proved only against him, or against Mr Bowes, that they have acted in the business after she was taken from Middlesex, and carried into the county of Durham, yet if from those acts you are of opinion they were privy to the design at first, that will warrant the

conclusion

conclusion that they are guilty also, but it is for you to draw that conclusion—if you should be of opinion that either of them were totally unacquainted with the business, till they found her in the county of Durham, I think in this case they ought to be acquitted, but if from their conduct afterwards, you are satisfied that they also were privy to the design before she was taken in the county of Middlesex, that will be sufficient to convict them also. With respect to Mr Thomas Bowes, it will be material for you to consider a little, what is his character and situation in life, it is proved that he is the attorney of Mr Bowes, the principal defendant, he had been concerned for him in his business some time before—he does not appear personally to have acted in this business till they got to Streatlam Castle—but he came there on Sunday, and in the middle of the night—he came into the room where Peter Orme slept, and he called Thomas—Thomas, says Orme, I am not Thomas—upon that he went into the next room where Chapman and Pigg lay, he staid some time, and they had a good deal of conversation, but the witness did not hear what it was, after this, says the witness, I took up some papers which had been put under the door, I shewed them to Mr Thomas Bowes—says he, put them where you found them, for I have nothing to do with it—says the witness, it was a paper with some writing upon it, I found it about nine. Then Mr Hobson tells you, that he saw Mr Thomas Bowes at Streatlam Castle—this was the time that Bowes was said to be ill there, and Bowes was denied to him—Bowes said he was afraid of his creditors—as for himself, he said, he had no conception, and he believes that Thomas Bowes knew no more of it than he did, he came on business, he said he wanted to see Mr Bowes on particular business—Bourn told him he could not be seen, and Bourn carried up the message, and he said he believed he was in the dark about it—says Hobson, I brought down a verbal message in order to deceive him. Thomas Ridgway said he got to Streatlam on the 13th of November, about three, he could not get admittance, he called out, and a gentleman came to the door, and said who do you want?—he said he wanted to speak to Mr Bowes, his name was Ridgway, and he was alone, and the gentleman, whom he since understands to be Mr. Thomas Bowes opened the window, and said Mr Bowes was not there, and he asked him how long he had been gone—to which he replied, I cannot hold any conversation with you on the subject, he waited there along while, and shoved the rule under the door, called out, and demanded Lady Strathmore a vast number of times, and he says, he thinks Mr Bowes was within hearing—it was possible he might hear. Christopher Stokel says, he carried a letter from Mr Bowes to Mr Thomas Bowes the day they came to Streatlam Castle, Bourn gave it him, and he delivered it to Mr Thomas Bowes at Darlington that he carried some Bank notes, and brought back threescore guineas, and Mr Farrer tells you, that Mr Thomas Bowes acted as the attorney to Mr Bowes, that he saw him at the Castle on the 16th of November, when he demanded the Lady as he did the day before, and that he told him, he should be sorry to commit any violence, but must break open the Castle, and when the people began to force the way, then a voice called out, I will let you in with one or two friends, which he supposes to be the voice of Mr Thomas Bowes, no other person being in the Hall, and upon his enquiring after Mr. Bowes and Lady Strathmore where they were—he said he had not seen them, and upon his more particularly addressing Mr. Bowes, and saying, Sir you certainly know where they are, he said, he would not answer any questions upon interrogatories. Then Robert Peverell tells you, that he saw Orme give a paper to Mr Thomas Bowes, and he said it must be put back again, and not be looked at, and he says, that Thomas Bowes did not mention any writ or pone to him at first, but afterwards he made terms that a pone should not come into the house. Gentlemen, these are all the witnesses that speak about Thomas Bowes. Mr Lee has been asked as to his knowledge, of Mr Thomas Bowes—he has known him for many years, and never knew a man of a fairer character—so it is as to the last defendant, Thomas Bowes, and first of all, on the cross-examination it has been endeavoured to lay facts before you, from whence you might conclude, that Mr Thomas Bowes, even in the part he acted at Streatlam Castle, was actuated by very different motives—not with a design or intent to assist Mr Bowes in the violence he might have against the person of Lady Strathmore and it has been proved, that as to one of the witnesses, he made an agreement with him, that he would not let him in unless he would engage, that no writ of pone should be exe-

M   cuted

cuted—the writ of poney you have heard is a writ in the county of Durham, by virtue of which the goods of the defendant are seized, in order to compel an appearance, but you have no evidence that any such writ ever existed, it is in evidence that the mob never collected, or came about the house, till the Tipstaff came, you are likewise told, he never saw Lady Strathmore in the house—if it is proved to you, that on the very day Mr Bowes comes down to Streatlam Castle, he writes to Thomas Bowes, his attorney, and he comes over—it will be for you to say, whether it is possible he should be ignorant she was there? If he knew she was in the house? the question is, whether that does not go a great way to prove what he pretended not to know? But you find by the evidence of Rippon, that even before they got there, he is in extreme anxiety about Mr. Bowes, and about some intelligence he was to receive from him—for he says to Rippon, he expected letters from Mr Bowes about the time of the fall, and therefore he ordered this witness to go every morning to the Post-office, to see if there were any letters—he is asked how do the letters from Streatlam come?—why not by the post, but by an old man by the name of Christopher—then what letter could Thomas Bowes expect? The question will be, whether on his evidence, and his conduct afterwards when he is in the house, and the secret manner in which he goes from room to room to the servants, whether on this evidence you are satisfied that he also was privy to the design?—if you are of that opinion you will find them all guilty,—you are to compare the evidence, and you will say whether there is any difference in the guilt of the defendants

The Jury, after a very few minutes consideration, and without retiring, (at half past four in the afternoon) brought in their verdict, ALL GUILTY *of the whole charge.*

THE

THE

JUDGMENT of the COURT,

WITH THE

ARGUMENTS of COUNSEL on giving the same.

ON Tuesday the 26th of June, 1787, Andrew Robinson Bowes, Esq; Edward Lucas, Francis Peacock, Mark Prevot, and Henry Bourn were brought up in custody of the Marshal of the King's Bench Prison, into the Court of King's Bench at Westminster, before the Judges sitting there, in order to receive sentence for the crime of which they had been convicted, when Mr. Justice Buller (after reading his report of the evidence before stated to have been given on the part of the prosecution) made the following observations on the five defendants above named —

The case of the seven first defendants in this cause, who were those acting in London, stood so circumstanced, that the Counsel at the trial very wisely left it on some general observations, for the case afforded no others.

With respect to the other two defendants, they were very ably defended, and the ground of their defence principally was, that they were never out of the county of Durham, the rule I laid down at the trial was this, that if the Jury, on the whole of the case, were of opinion, that they were totally unapprised of the business till Lady Strathmore was actually found in the county of Durham, I thought they should find them not guilty, but if from their conduct afterwards, they were satisfied that they also were privy to the design, before she was taken in the county of Middlesex, in that case they were all equally guilty, only one witness was called on the part of the defendants, which was Mr. Lee, who said he had known Mr Thomas Bowes many years, and known him in business pretty frequently, and known a good deal of his reputation, and never knew any man in the profession that bore a fairer or more honourable character. On this case the Jury found all the defendants guilty, and I think there are five of them appear, and I will therefore state a little how these five stand.—Mr Bowes himself stands in a situation that requires no comment,—there is Francis Peacock, who, I think, appears by the evidence, to have been with Mr Bowes so early as October, is proved to be a man acting in the business from that time to the moment Lady Strathmore was carried off,—the next is Mr Bourn, who was servant to Mr Bowes, who lived at Streatlam Castle, and it does not appear he was out of the county of Durham at all,—the next is Mark Prevot, who was Mr Bowes's servant, and attended him during the whole business,—the only remaining man is Lucas. Now Lucas is certainly proved to be a constable, a peace officer, and minister of the public justice of the country, he has availed himself of that character, in order to carry this plot into execution—it is not probable that any man but a peace officer could have carried this plan into execution, which we have heard of. Besides this, it appears on the evidence, that Lucas had insinuated himself into the good opinion of Lady Strathmore under the mask of friendship—that he offered himself to her as assistant—he enlisted himself into her pay, and actually received her money down to the hour she was taken off.—There is likewise this strong evidence for saying that this man was the contriver of the whole business—he assembles them all together, before they went to make the affidavit upon which they took up the coachman and footman; and therefore there is strong reason to suppose he was privy to that perjury committed by Chapman—Chapman was carried

before

before Mr Walker, at whose office this man attended, when he gets to Forster's, where Lady Strathmore is, he gets her to open the door, telling her, that her friend Lucas was come—by that treachery he got admission to her, and it seems to me, that there never was any conduct in which the character of a peace officer has been so abused as by him, at the voice of a constable, and at his appearance, every man opens his doors with perfect confidence, knowing that both his person and property will be protected from violence—the most hardened offender submits to his authority, because he is sure, that as far as concerns the security of his person he shall be protected, this man, who in words had mocked and insulted Lady Strathmore, by pretending to protect her, was the very man who took her in this manner till he saw her locked up safe within the walls of her own Castle.

Mr ERSKINE We wish to pray your Lordships to have an opportunity of answering those observations which the Counsel for the Crown shall make on our affidavits, and then the Crown is not deprived of the liberty of answering those arguments, by way of reply, this I take, my Lords, to be the order of your proceedings.

Mr MINGAY On the part of the Crown, I believe the practice to be directly contrary, it is always of course for the Counsel on the part of the defendant to read their affidavits, if they have any, then the Counsel for the Crown to make their observations.

Mr JUSTICE ASHURST. If they produce affidavits, and you should answer them, then to be sure it is fit they should begin first

Mr MINGAY On the part of the Crown, I certainly pray that you will pass a very heavy sentence on these persons now before the Court, if my learned friend Mr Erskine has nothing to say in mitigation

Mr. ERSKINE I am not perfectly understood—I wish to know whether the other learned Counsel who attend on the part of the Crown have any thing further to offer, because I take it for granted, that every man must have an opportunity of answering what is alledged, else why stand here as Counsel, if therefore my learned friend Mr Law, and the others, if they have any thing to alledge, I trust I shall have an opportunity of answering it

Mr LAW In the case of the King and Bowman there was the same objection made, and it was ordered to go on.

Mr ERSKINE However the evidence may be distorted in observation, I am here without any probability of making a reply

Mr JUSTICE ASHURST But the Counsel certainly cannot answer the affidavits before they have heard them

Mr ERSKINE I am intirely in the judgment of the Court

Mr JUSTICE BULLER. You should produce the affidavits first, and they should be opened, but I do not know that any rule has been settled whether they are intitled to two speeches or one

Mr. GARROW In the King and Aylett they spoke in extenuation first

Mr JUSTICE ASHURST Then Mr Erskine open what your affidavits are

Mr JUSTICE GROSE The Counsel for the Crown have no affidavits to read in aggravation

Mr ERSKINE None at all.

MR. ERSKINE IN MITIGATION.

My Lords,

IN representing the different persons who appear before your Lordships to day, I wish to put myself, if possible, in the same temper of mind which they ought to be in, when they stand before your Lordships, with all that humiliation which becomes them, therefore, I purpose so to manage this matter, knowing that whether I speak first, or whether I speak last—whether I have an opportunity of replying or not before this business is finished, the Court will be perfectly in possession of all that can be said in point of defence, before I proceed to state those circumstances which I am humbly to offer to the Court in mitigation of the sentence, it is necessary that I should consider what sort of evidence it is, that it is for me to comment upon, and I apprehend there is no principle clearer or better understood than this, that you will not presume any fact is found by the Jury, except such as are necessary to support their verdict, and that all those facts which have been given in evidence before the Jury, and which have

received

received perfect credit both from the Jury and the Court, could not in point of law have changed that verdict, when I confider the fituation of my unfortunate clients, particularly fome of them, I confefs it is a peculiar fatisfaction to me, that the manner in which the caufe was conducted at the trial received the approbation of the learned Judge, and I feel myfelf very much obliged to that learned Judge for publickly expreffing that approbation, it does relieve me from that load of anxiety which I hope always to feel when the happinefs and comfort, and fuccefs of others depend on my feeble endeavours I thought it very much my duty in decency, in refpect to the public order, and the laws of the country, to forbear offering any circumftances, which however they could not tend to alter the verdict, might have operated as a fnare to the confciences of the Jury, and might have mifled the public, but though they never could in juftice change the verdict, yet they may very much change the fentence to-day. If therefore in the courfe of the trial, I could have fhewn that Mr Bowes conceived the plan of carrying Lady Strathmore from her fituation—not for the purpofe of ftopping that fuit—not by perpetual imprifonment—not by removing her from the poffibility of profecuting that fuit, but becaufe it was impoffible for him to withdraw her from the confpiracy that had been practifed on both their happinefs, if I could have proved, my Lords, that after they had gone two ftages from London fhe was perfectly reconciled—if I could have proved that fhe embraced Mr Bowes as her deliverer, why, my Lords, your Lordfhips know very well that could not change the verdict, becaufe however proper Mr. Bowes's conduct might have been, he muft purfue fuch conduct in legal courfes, he certainly ftands before your Lordfhips, whatever may be faid in mitigation, truly and juftly in that refpect convicted, this therefore is the proper feafon to lay before you all the motives that produced this conduct, but before I go to that part of the cafe, it will be neceffary to diftinguifh the fituation of the different defendants—I am certainly not moving for a new trial—I am certainly not faying you are to pronounce no judgment on Mr Bourn, yet it feems that the evidence on which he is convicted is of fo flight and doubtful a nature, fo hardly within the bounds and limits of law, even taken for true, that you will feel the impreffion of that doubt, it appears that he was never within two hundred miles of this fcene of oppreffion—it appears that Mr Bowes never communicated to him his intention of carrying off this Lady—it does not appear directly or indirectly, that he was guilty of one overt act in this confpiracy, but the utmoft is, that which I hardly think is a crime in England, a fpecies of mifprifion, that he knew the plan of Mr Bowes, that he was acquainted with his intention of going back to London, from acting in concert with Hobfon, in the fuppofed fall, and from his afterwards fuffering Mr Bowes to take a chaife, in the profecution of this bufinefs, in the county of Durham. The Jury were to collect from thence an overt act of confpiracy, I apprehend that if it appears to the Court, that upon the evidence Bourn ought not to have been convicted, you will pronounce no fentence upon him, or at leaft a nominal one In a queftion of civil profecution, where no new trial is moved for, you muft confirm the verdict of the Jury, and the profecutrix is entitled to the fruit of that verdict, but when your Lordfhips fit there to pronounce a difcretionary judgment, I take it for granted that you will pronounce no judgment, if you fee either that this man's conduct ftands on fuch doubtful evidence that he cannot be fuppofed to be guilty, or that that is not founded in law, in either of thefe cafes I hope you will pronounce no fentence on Mr Bourn I take it that there is nothing more clear than this, that to warrant a conviction againft Mr Bourn, on an information filed with the venue laid in Middlefex, that he muft have been guilty of fome overt act of confpiracy in that county, and that the Jury muft have been able to collect from evidence fuch overt act, now the utmoft that could be inferred is, that the Judge told the Jury they were warranted to infer, that he knew of the intention of Mr Bowes in October, that he concealed that intention, and that he abetted it, but where did he abet it? He abetted it, if at all, in the county of Durham: there is no evidence, directly or indirectly, that he was prefent when Lady Strathmore complained fhe was under durefs, there was only one circumftance of that kind under the gate of the caftle, and then Bourn was not prefent, he fees her therefore in the poffeffion of her hufband, he fees her in his poffeffion, apparently, with her confent, it is, therefore, reduced to this dry point of law, this is an abetting to an act to be carried into effect, contrary to law, in the county of Middlefex, by a perfon locally in the county of Durham, never going out of that county. Does that warrant a

conviction

conviction of any perfon in the county of Middlefex? Now is Bourn to efcape from
juftice altogether, or now to be convicted? I anfwer thus, after the conviction of
Bowes and his other affociates in London, Bourn might have been convicted by information filed, or an indictment, in that county, charging him with an overt act of
confpiracy in the county of Middlefex, and it feems to me to be an abolition of
that local judicature, which has been immemorial in this country, and, I apprehend,
if this had been an overt act of high treafon, if it appeared that he had always
been perfonally prefent in the county of Durham, that he could not have been tried
with the other defendants, whofe acts of confpiracy were properly laid in the county
of Middlefex. But, leaving that to the Court, in the firft place, for againft Bourn
the evidence is extremely flight, and, my Lords, I hope it is no part of the principle
of the law of England, that guilt is to be prefumed, intended, or inferred, I apprehend the contrary is the cafe, and that it is neceffary to faften on Bourn fome
overt act of the crime with which he was charged, of confpiring to imprifon this
lady, on the 10th of November, in the county of Middlefex, now what is there?
Nothing, but that Mr Bowes having told Bourn, as he fwears pofitively in his affidavit, that if he could only gain the fmalleft opportunity to fee Lady Strathmore,
he could defeat the defigns of his enemies, that all his paths were watched and
marked, and that the only chance he had, was, by having it fuppofed that he was ill,
and to take a private journey to London, and that he defired him to go to Hobfon to
fetch him, the only evidence againft Bourn is, that he abetted this deceit of Mr
Bowes, in faying that he had fallen from his horfe, Mr Bowes pofitively fwearing
before your Lordfhips to day, that he never did communicate to Bourn any fuch intention, and Bourn declaring that he never had any conception of fuch intention, and
that when he faw her at the caftle, he faw nothing that led him to believe her to
be there, otherwife than by her own confent. My Lord, Mr Bourn ftands in another predicament, he was a fervant to Mr Bowes, you will not wifh to break that
domeftic confidence, unlefs Mr Bowes had been carrying on fomething againft the
government of the ftate, in that cafe the duty to the government fuperfedes all
others, but I cannot think it is proper that the moment a fervant has reafon to
fuppofe his mafter is about to be guilty of fome petty crime, that the inftant
he is engaged in fome act which the law will not juftify, he is to be dragged to
punifhment, becaufe he does not behave with that decency or propriety, which
his fervant may think neceffary. If Bourn had been a mere ftranger, officioufly
practifing this deceit, you would have prefumed every thing againft him, but here
is the fubordination which a fervant ought to ufe to his mafter, that he
does thofe things by his command, his mafter may not communicate to him
his object, Mr Bowes fwears he did not, Bourn confirms that affidavit, by
fwearing he did not fee, or know of his plan, and under thefe circumftances, the
evidence being fo very flight, I hope you will be very mild in your
Lordfhip's fentence on Mr Bourn. Permit me to add, my Lords, that he
is an agent for annuitants in the county of Durham, he has a large family, and you
will expofe his family to abfolute ruin, if he is imprifoned in the King's Bench or
in Newgate, for how is it poffible for him to continue fteward to the annuitants on
the eftate, and then he is deprived of his bread and his family turned out of doors.
I do hope that the Court, before they fubject a man to fo much mifery, to fo much
fhame, will fee that the judgment ftands on a clear and unequivocal foundation:
the fame reafon may be affigned for Mark Prevot, he is a fervant to Mr. Bowes, ob-
ferving his commands, a foreigner, a ftranger to our conftitution and laws, and ob-
ferving literally what his mafter commanded. With refpect to Mr. Bowes himfelf,
he ftands in a very delicate fituation, and I feel I ftand in fuch a fituation too, it
became neceffary at leaft for my learned friend and myfelf to leave it to him to
take this matter upon himfelf, and he offers thefe affidavits, and though I do not
think he is offering to you any matter which can poffibly aggravate his fentence, but
much which will go in mitigation, yet when thefe affidavits come to be read, there
are circumftances contained in them which you will eafily fee go beyond that difcretion, which, in my humble opinion, a counfel ought to affume, but then you
will confider how far it is fit and proper, and in what fituation Mr. Bowes found
himfelf to force him to difclofe thefe things to your Lordfhip that was for his
determination, and not for ours. If Lady Strathmore had confined her application
to the Courts of this country, to her own fecurity, this matter would never have
appeared, and you will fee in her hufband much defire to conceal it, but when fhe
comes

comes here for vengeance, if a man is so sorely pressed, it is not a wonder if he should turn in his own protection, and strip this lady of the mask in which she has so long walked, that of an oppressed and persecuted woman, he tells me and his other counsel that there is another tribunal to which, as a man of honor and feeling, he is amenable, namely, the great tribunal of the public, and although no man can indure not to state what were his sufferings, or what were the motives of his conduct, if it was to a woman that had all along conducted herself properly, yet in this case I am to state to you, with much reluctance, the matter contained in these affidavits. Mr Bowes states, (but before I mention any part of the affidavits, I will only make this observation) during the time I have had the honor to attend the court, I have had occasion to cite several cases which seemed to me to mark out very accurately the power of a husband in this country, and I apprehend it was decided in one of those cases in the King's Bench, that if a husband saw his wife conducting herself improperly, it was part not only of the power and authority of her husband, but part of his duty also to rescue her, and bring her back to that control, which, by the law, he has over her as a protector, and I apprehend in the most material part of these affidavits Mr Bowes is confirmed by other persons, and you will think, I am persuaded, that it was only the public justice of this country that required him to act as he did, without regarding what is said by these gentlemen Mr Bowes states his marriage in October 1777, he says he found out soon after his marriage that Lady Strathmore had conveyed away her estates to trustees, for her own separate use, this certainly does not place that Lady (I am sure I speak every thing of her with reluctance) in a very honourable light before the Court, but that is nothing to what is about to be stated

Mr. Justice ASHURST The Court must desire that you will abstain from going into any evidence but such as is relevant to this now before the Court—this passed ten years ago

Mr ERSKINE I apprehend this will be material, whatever the Court are disposed to do with this I am perfectly satisfied, but I cannot submit that the rigor of any imprisonment should be increased and aggravated by any reflection in Mr Bowes's own mind, that he has failed through me, this bears on the judgment you are to give this day, it is to shew your Lordships the situation of this Lady, and the circumstances under which she stood at the time he did this act, for which he is called to receive judgment, it is to shew in answer to that cruelty which is imputed to him, the various acts of tenderness of which his whole life has been composed, since his marriage, and the particular reasons why he was bound in honor and in compassion to her, to do the act which he has done Mr Justice Buller recollects, that when I proposed some evidence of this sort at the trial, it was at first over ruled, afterwards the judge was ready to receive it, but I then said that I was conscious if it was then produced it could not alter the verdict.

Mr. Justice BULLER. No, that was more confined than this you talk of now, that evidence was at the moment he took her away, not ten years past

Mr ERSKINE Is not it necessary to shew the situation of this Lady ? You certainly will take the whole of this gentleman's motives, they might depend on all these circumstances which I state, and certainly if they do not tend to mitigate, you will not give a mitigating sentence

Mr Justice GROSE You are opening certain transactions by Lady Strathmore, how does that tend to mitigate the punishment Mr Bowes is going to receive for conspiring to get her to drop the divorce ? For the thing you are opening would seem to make it rather a desirable thing, provided the circumstances warranted him in so doing

Mr. ERSKINE He is charged with cruelty towards this lady, I think any thing that shews nine years of tenderness, of forgiveness, of forbearance towards this Lady operates strongly to shew that is not true

Mr. Justice ASHURST We cannot receive it—Your own judgment must have told you so.

Mr MINGAY How is Lady Strathmore or we to answer her life and conversation for so many years past

Mr CHAMBRE The evidence now offered before the Court, is to lay before the Court the situation of this Lady up to the time of this business

Mr. Justice GROSE. How does that mitigate the enormity of this crime ?

Mr.

Mr CHAMBRE. To shew the absolute necessity he was under of securing her in some way or other

Mr. Justice GROSE. What to prevent a divorce?

Mr. Justice ASHURST It is neither more nor less than abusing the situation he is in, and taking an opportunity of publishing a gross libel.

Mr. LAW. When read it will form a very considerable degree of aggravation.

Mr. MINGAY. Suppose a man is brought up for a common assault a month ago, are you to give a history of the prosecutor's conduct, how many times he was convicted of robberies and other things?

Mr. Justice BULLER The Court are of opinion not to receive it.

Mr. MINGAY. It is calumny added to injustice.

Mr. GARROW. It will not be permitted to us to go into Mr. Bowes's character for ten years

Mr. Justice GROSE. I would rather the Counsel for Mr. Bowes should take upon themselves to say and act accordingly.

Mr. ERSKINE I have done my duty

Mr. Justice BULLER. I am of opinion now that that rule which I laid down when I corrected what I said at first was a true one, that you may be permitted to read affidavits of any thing that passed as to the immediate cause of taking her.

Mr. ERSKINE Mr. Bowes considers this as one of the immediate causes, is not a husband bound to protect his wife, and if she is not capable of governing and protecting herself, is he to suffer her to be in the hands of conspirators and servants?

Mr Justice GROSE. But you should confine yourself to these facts that were the immediate causes of his conspiring.

Mr. ERSKINE. They are so coupled and blended together, that I cannot state a part of the circumstances that led Mr. Bowes to do this, without stating the whole together.

Mr. Justice BULLER. The consequence of that is, that no part of your affidavit can be read.

Mr. GARROW. This would have been proper at the trial, it is improper here.

Mr Justice GROSE It would have been improper every where.

Mr GARROW. The Jury certainly have found all these motives.

Mr. ERSKINE. It is perfectly consistent with the verdict of the Jury.

Mr. J. ASHURST. The Court put off the bringing up Mr Bowes in order that you might read the affidavits and weed them of any matter improper, and if you have not made use of that discretion, or if your client has not permitted you to do it, they cannot be read.

Mr. ERSKINE. I have now discharged part of my duty to Mr. Bowes, and he will see that it is the Court that have prevented my concluding that duty, I therefore now confine myself to that matter which certainly you must think immediately applies to the subject, and was the immediate cause, the first fact stated on the affidavit was this deed which she had before her marriage made in trust for her own separate use; she made afterwards another deed, which had for its object the destruction of that, there was a counter-part of this deed kept secretly, by a person of the name of Walker, and there was a conspiracy between a person of the name of George Walker, Mary Morgan, and one Susannah Church, to cause Lady Strathmore to elope from her husband, with whom she was living, at that time, in perfect harmony and peace; they carried her to the house of one Mr. Shuter, who, as I understand, is a barrister at law, where she went under the name of Mrs Jeffries, this was done immediately after the proceedings of the Court of Chancery, to gratify Lady Strathmore, yet, notwithstanding the harmony in which they were living at that time, on a sudden, but entirely owing to them, as it is stated by Susannah Church herself; she was carried to Mr Shuter's house, and it was agreed among themselves that Mrs. Morgan should be the manager of her affairs, that all her estates were secured by the counter-part of this deed, and that she was rid of Mr. Bowes for ever, Mr. Bowes found Lady Strathmore was exposed to most cruel hardships by those people, that kept her as if she had been a lunatic, that she was so confined that she

was

was hardly allowed to go from one room to another, and those facts do not stand alone upon the affidavit of Mr. Bowes, but Susannah Church, one of the persons entrusted to carry this conspiracy into effect, comes before you on an affidavit, and states the whole of it, now I submit whether, under these circumstances, Mr Bowes has not something to offer in mitigation of his punishment for taking her into his possession, for taking her into his own hands, he tells us if she had been under the protection of her own relations, if she had been visited and protected by them, he never would have interfered to stop that free agency, which she had in bringing this divorce before the Commons, but he swears that the suits in the Commons were carrying on against him by conspiracy, to ruin the peace of Lady Strathmore and himself, under these circumstances, is it to be wondered at that Mr Bowes should want to get her back, and that, coupled by these circumstances, which, as they are now concealed from the eye of the Court, I shall not endeavour to introduce, that he did endeavour to rescue her from that injury and misery, and that that was the original cause of endeavouring to take away Lady Strathmore   The evidence is reported by the learned judge in his detail of the various artifices and stratagems by which it was carried into effect, but you will look at the motives, and will not think it very material the manner in which it was carried into execution, except that part of it which has already fallen under the animadversion of the Court   Mr Bowes swears that he never threatened Lady Strathmore, as stated by some of the witnesses on the trial—that he never treated her with any indecency or violence—that the great object he had was to conciliate her affections, if he had meant to imprison her he would have carried her beyond the seas, out of the reach of the Court, instead of that he carried her to the castle of her ancestors, where he had no authority, amongst her relations and friends, and where she had every opportunity of redress, his only motive for seeking to have her in his possession was to have an opportunity of beating down that conspiracy against him, and of reconciling her by gentleness and tenderness, which it will appear, by the affidavits, he used   I have affidavits which it will be necessary to shew to the Court, in which it will appear, that she behaved with good humour, and that she was reciprocally satisfied, if that appears, it places Mr Bowes in a different situation from that which he stands in on the trial, and if I had given it in evidence on the trial, the Court has said, it would not have altered the verdict, there is one part of the evidence very material to attend to, that is the part which Mr Bowes took in those acts which Mr Lucas stands charged with before the Court, because, if you, on the whole of the case, should be of opinion that Mr Bowes, finding his wife was under the dominion of persons who sought to keep up this disunion, if he believed he could defeat that conspiracy, if he believed he would have an opportunity of living with her on the same terms he originally had, it will alter the punishment, provided he does not appear to have acted corruptly and unwarrantably in the manner in which he acted.   With respect to the oath taken before the Justice of the Peace, Mr Bowes gives this account, in which he is confirmed by Lucas himself, and a person of the name of Dove—he denies that he ever did instigate any person to take a false oath, and had no knowledge that any such warrant had been issued or applied for, till the evening of the 9th of November, when Lucas informed him that John Cummins had been threatened to be murdered, and got a warrant against them   Mr Bowes blames Lucas, Lucas assures him he had done nothing but what was legal and proper, he had no notion that Cummins was not threatened, and Dove swears he was present, and Lucas says the application to Walker for the warrant, and the obtaining of the warrant, was without any knowledge of Mr Bowes, who, to the best of his recollection, expressed his disapprobation of it, and it certainly is extremely material, if Mr Bowes can rescue himself from that part of the transaction, then his offence will be reduced to having taken away Lady Strathmore in a manner which the law could not warrant, for, to be sure, though a husband is entitled to the possession of his wife, he must not do it in a manner that is illegal, but there is a vast deal of difference between stratagem and fraud, and acting contrary to the law.   Now with respect to Lucas something is to be said in mitigation of his punishment, Mr. Bowes, who seems to have had a very generous and proper anxiety to speak the whole truth, even against himself, where it tends to hurt others, says, and Lucas says the same, that Mr Bowes told him that Lady Strathmore had carried off a great quantity of diamonds, and he desired Lucas to get possession of Lady Strathmore, in order to recover them. Mr Bowes is ready to take upon himself any consequence that shall

O   follow

follow from that, Lucas then being entirely ignorant of the real defign of Mr Bowes, and fancying he was about to take her into custody for recovering these diamonds, and swearing that he did not know he was carying off Lady Strathmore for the reafon Mr Bowes communicated to him —he fays that Cummins informed him he had been fo threatened by the friends of Lady Strathmore, that they faid they would murder her, that he did advife Cummins to take out this warrant, but did not advife him to take a falfe oath—fo far in mitigation of the conduct of Lucas, but, as it affects Mr Bowes, furely it is extremely material for him, confirmed by Lucas himfelf, who difclofes this, that it was merely the act of Lucas taking this perfon into custody on the information of Cummins, that Mr Bowes had no hand in it, that he approved of it at erwards, and in fhort that it is chargeable upon him. With refpect to Peacock, I have an affidavit from him alfo—he appears to be a gentleman, in long intimacy with Mr Bowes refiding at Newcastle, a man, I underftand, who has preferved a pretty good character, and he pofitively fwears, that till the time they were in the coach, for the purpofe of taking Lady Strathmore, Mr Bowes never told him the reafon, that he attended Mr Bowes to give him pecuniary affiftance, and he withdraws himfelf from every thing, except that one of going with Lady Strathmore, he ftands merely before the Court, as a perfon who unfortunately was prefent in his coach, not having it communicated to him till the very moment it was carried into execution; it appears by Peacock's affidavit, that he was not prefent at the time Lady Strathmore was taken, and that he did not fhove her into the coach. My Lords, I have now ftated all that I recollect, concerning Mr Bowes, and Bourn, who was in his fervice. Peacock, and Prevot the laft witneſs, Chapman, Figg and Bickley, are not before the Court, and Mr Thomas Bowes, they do not, at prefent, prefs fentence againft, under all thefe circumftances I hope, from hearing the affidavits you will be difpofed to think Mr Bowes is not fo criminal as he appears on the report of the learned Judge. I have already explained why this matter did not appear at the trial—if, on the whole, you fhould think Mr Bowes found that there was a confpiracy againft him to withdraw Lady Strathmore without any crime—that fhe was, in fact, not a free agent, but under the dominion of others—that he conceived he could defeat thefe effects, and make her live in happinefs and comfort, and that ftanding in fuch a relation as he did, he certainly could not confpire againft his intereft, I truft the punifhment will not be of that fort which you would be difpofed to inflict, if thefe affidavits were not offered to the confideration of the Court. It is further remarkable, that during the time that this lady lived feparate from her hufband, fhe was living with thofe whom Mr Bowes fuppofed were making a prey of her, for that furely is material, and the difficulty I feel is how to mention one without bringing the other before the Court

Mr J Ashurst. As to any part of Mr Bowes's affidavit we cannot fuffer it to be read—we cannot read any of it without fileing it in Court—fuch a piece of flander ought not to remain on the files of this Court, he might have had an opportunity—his Counfel muft know the Court could not receive it—if he will take this opportunity of conveying that fcandal and impertinence to the world, he deferves not to have his affidavit read.

Mr Erskine. He is placed in a hard fituation, becaufe all that I fay goes for nothing, if thefe affidavits are to be drawn from under me

Mr J Ashurst. Then you have drawn them from under yourfelf, or your client has withdrawn them from you, and you muft thank yourfelf, if he will be fo obftinate as not to be advifed, he muft take the confequences

Mr Fielding. I conceived this, that if the punifhment of thefe things was prefcribed by act of Parliament, that then it would not have been neceffary to have fet before the Court the motives, but when you are to adminifter difcretionary punifhment, I conceived you would have enquired into all the circumftances of the cafe, it was upon that idea I own, that I concurred in thefe affidavits being prefented to the Court

Mr Mingay. I have no objection to take it for granted, that every thing that is fworn, the Court ought to receive as fworn, and that it is as Mr. Erfkine has mentioned.

Mr J Buller. You are acceding to every thing that they wifh, but it cannot be fuffered to remain on the files of the Court, fuch affidavits as thefe.

Mr Mingay. I have no doubt but he has fworn all thefe things, and in my opinion they aggravate his crime.

Mr.

M. ERSKINE I will put in these affidavits of Peacock's that I mentioned—in the mean time, Mr Bowes may in ten words say what I conceive may be material for him in this case   (*The several affidavits were then read*)

M CHAMBRE On the part of Bourn, Peacock, and Prevot, as the several grounds of mitigation, have been so fully stated to the Court by Mr Erskine, it renders it unnecessary I should take up much of the time of the Court, and I shall begin with the circumstances of Mr Bourn's case, and whether I look at the affidavits produced by him in mitigation of the sentence now about to be passed, or whether I look at the evidence, I find myself much at a loss to account for the verdict of the Jury against him—most undoubtedly I must consider that verdict as properly founded   but if it appears to the Court under all the circumstances of the case, that the verdict is a very hard one—I may say, an improper one—the Court will let his sentence be as mild as possible   I take it to be clear, that no man ought to be convicted of any offence but upon evidence applicable to that specific offence, and I do not find any evidence that Bourn was privy to, or had any connection with this proceeding, with respect to the only material circumstance that happened in the county previous to that catastrophe, it consisted merely of the sham fall and the false report that was given out to the public, with respect to the injury received, the evidence which was laid before you as far as it went, certainly tended to prove that Bourn was not apprised of it, Mr Hobson, the principal witness who spoke to the fact said, he himself, to whom it was communicated, was deceived—Mr Thomas Bowes was deceived, and he believed Bourn was deceived with respect to that transaction, that act in itself was not a criminal act, and not being a criminal act, there is no reason why the Court should apply any part of Bourn's conduct in that transaction, to the transaction which is the subject of this information   The only ostensible motive of Mr Bowes was a wish to be concealed, particularly from his creditors, it is not proved, either directly, or by any circumstance, that Bourn knew one tittle beyond that in which it was not in Bourn's situation to control his master at that time, and it will hardly be expected of him to dissuade his master from that act, it seems to be just as absurd, as to suppose that if a man that committed a robbery in one county, that it is probable that he has committed murder in another, it is in express terms denied by Bourn, and he is confirmed by Mr Bowes, that he was not privy to his intention at that time, after the return of Mr Bowes, it does not appear in evidence that Bourn knew there was any restraint on the person of Lady Strathmore—it does not appear that in his hearing, or to his knowledge, she expressed the smallest disapprobation on her part—he was going on other business, and had no privity at all with the matter, with respect to the subject on which he is supposed to give intelligence of what passed at Darlington, and that he took an active part in assisting Mr Bowes to make his escape—he swears he did not go on any such purpose, that his business was the proper business of his office, which he held under Mr Bowes, that he had been collecting rents, and met Mr Bowes merely by accident, when Mr Bowes required of him the use of his horse—certainly it is that in this particular case with respect to Mr Bourn, nothing is imputable to him with respect to the peculiar manner in which the conspiracy was carried into execution—Mr Bourn was, for any thing that appears in evidence, and by his own affidavit, which is still more, certainly not at all apprised of any intention that an improper use would be made of any legal process—certainly was not privy to any acts of cruelty and violence against Lady Strathmore, if any such were in truth committed—thus he stands as innocent as any man not in the act, the case in respect being thus circumstanced with respect to him, there being no positive evidence of any improper act in the county of Durham, the Court will consider him guilty of a very insignificant offence indeed—The case of Prevot certainly seems to be intitled to a great deal of the favour of the Court—Prevot is not affected by any particular circumstance of the conspiracy, only that he attended them on the journey in his character as servant, and was not privy to any one act of violence—he attended his master's carriage, which he conceived at that time to be his duty to do—as man is a foreigner, a stranger to the customs and laws of the country, he naturally conceived he was not liable to any punishment whatever in attending his master, he could not conceive he had any right, power, or authority whatever to control the acts of his master, and no acts of violence are said to be proved to affect this person   and in the case of Peacock his defence rises more from his own affidavit, and from the affidavit which Mr Bowes has made on his behalf, than from the evidence in this cause, the evidence in this cause takes up Peacock at an earlier part of this transaction, and there were certain circumstances proper to be laid before a Jury, and to be taken by them into confideration, and they have thought proper to convict him, and Peacock expresly fwears, and is confirmed in that, that he was not privy to the intention of Mr Bowes, till the very morning of this transaction—he was apprized of Mr Bowes's wifh to remain concealed from his creditors, he was a perfon with whom Mr Bowes had long been in habits of intimacy and friendfhip, they had lived much together, Peacock was ufeful to him in his affairs, he was privy to moft of them, he fwears, and he is confirmed by Mr Bowes, that the only motive to fecret him was the apprehenfion of an arreft fiom his creditors, in confequence of his fituation, this is exprefsly fworn to by Peacock, till the very morning when that tranfaction happened, and he accompanied him no further than the town of Stamford, again him therefore there is no evidence of privity, or acts of violence, he difclaims any knowledge of fuch, any belief of fuch, on the contrary, he had great reafon to believe that Mr. Bowes's motive was to effect a reconciliation, and that he had every reafon to believe that the fcheme of Mr Bowes, if it had taken effect, would have worked a reconciliation, for fo far from perceiving any difinclination, he perceived expreffions of fondnefs and endearment, and was fully convinced that Mr Bowes's previous information had been well founded, and that if by means of the communication he had been able to get Lady Strathmore into his poffeffion, fhe fhould be reconciled, and all differences would be at an end. This is the ftate of the cafe with refpect to Peacock, which ought certainly to diminifh his punifhment, with refpect to Mr. Bowes, whatever motives of delicacy or difcretion might have difpofed him to forbear going into all the circumftances of Lady Strathmore's fituation, I certainly had conceived it was competent to him to fhew by any circumftance that could apply to the fact—what his motives were, for moft undoubtedly the motives that induce any man to act in a cafe where there is no punifhment affixed by the law, muft have great weight when they are going to pafs that punifhment, but the Court has decided otherwife, and though that decifion has certainly cut off a very confiderable part of the evidence on the part of Mr Bowes, I truft that fufficient remains to fhew that Mr. Bowes was not actuated by thofe motives imputed to him on the part of the profecution, but though he has acted indifcreetly, though he has acted wrong, though he has acted in violation of the law, yet he has fo done under fuch motives as will furnifh a very material ground of mitigation; it appears that Mr Bowes had information fiom his own oath, and from the oath of Sufannah Church, that Lady Strathmore after her elopement was under a degree of reftraint for a month, or a greater fpace of time, that fhe was conftantly in tears, expreffing her unhappinefs, and under a very confiderable degree of reftraint and control, that was a circumftance that would have juftified a hufband in enquiring into it, it would not juftify him in taking thofe methods of obtaining fatisfaction which he has unfortunately purfued, but had he purfued other modes which might have been prefcribed, it certainly would have been a juftification, the information was fuch as could not deceive him, it was the information of thofe that lived under the fame roof, and faw what was paffing, befides that, the matter ftated in the affidavit, and which I am fure it is not in my wifh to repeat, was certainly fuch as would have juftified a hufband in taking his wife into his cuftody, and to have impofed upon her a very confiderable degree of reftraint, there are cafes which would have warranted that, not that he would have been warranted in taking any meafure to have ftopped the fuit, but independent of that circumftance, he would have been well juftified in taking her, and taking her againft her will, into his poffeffion, and keeping her under a very confiderable degree of reftraint. Mr Bowes has very fully explained his motive, he has fworn that thofe motives induced him to purfue that conduct which he has unfortunately purfued; and with refpect to every circumftance of cruelty it is exprefsly denied, and it is proved by feveral of the affidavits that have been read, that there certainly was on a great variety of occafions, every appearance of reconciliation. with refpect to that which conftituted a confiderable part of his crime, if it had been left unexplained, I mean the circumftance of obtaining a warrant, I conceive Mr. Bowes is fully exculpated from that, for it is exprefsly fworn by him, and denied by a perfon prefent, and by the very perfon who committed that tranfaction, that denial is accompanied with circumftances of difapprobation, and it was not till after ftrong affurances that the complaint was founded in truth, that Mr Bowes confented to the improper ufe of it, the ufe was certainly improper, but the knowledge of it easly denied, if Mr. Bowes had meant to have imposed a perpetual restraint on the person of Lady Strathmore, nothing was so obvious as to have carried her out of the kingdom, it was extremely easy to effectuate that purpose, but it does not appear that he had that purpose in view, if that had been his object he most undoubtedly never would have carried her to her own estate, in the midst of her fortune, in the midst of persons dependent on her and her family, and who had been in the habits of attention and respect to that family and herself, but he did carry her there, and she appeared on several occasions publickly there, and he swears positively that if he found himself unable to prevail upon her to consent to live with him by fair means, it was his intention to restore her to the custody of those friends whom she chose, yet he swears that was his determined resolution, if by fair means he could not prevail upon her to live with him, but that was his determined resolution, if he possibly could. My Lords, under these circumstances I hope many of the most material parts that compose the aggravation are entirely done away, Mr Bowes has been rash, unfortunate in those means which appeared to him to be laudable, and which have subjected him to the censure of this Court, that censure he himself submits to, and I trust that that judgment which unexplained might have been very severe, will be extenuated to a very considerable degree

Mr. FIELDING. My Lords, although I am on the same side, I hope I shall be forgiven for taking up a short portion of your Lordship's time, the subject on which I have to address you has certainly been sufficiently exhausted, and every thing said upon it that the ingenuity of the gentlemen could suggest. My Lords, I am sure your Lordships will all think of the situation of those defendants with undisturbed temper, and indeed from the particular turn this cause has taken to which I bow, that the affidavits should not be read in the manner they were intended to be read, I am the more inclined to consider this case as a public crime (if indeed it is capable of that decisive idea) it may be taken up as a crime, which it imports you to punish as an offence against the publick, if it is to be considered with any relation to those that are suffering under it, then it seems that circumstance of the affidavit, explaining the motive, would be more material than the circumstances are in a public crime demanding a public punishment according to the injury the public might experience, if that is the way in which it is to be considered, and it seems to me to be the proper way, it would not make that question very material, whether the Counsel for the defendants were to be heard first, or the gentlemen on the other side, if that were not the case, it certainly would have been extremely cruel on the present occasion, for if after precluding Mr Bowes from all possible circumstances of extenuation, it was open to the gentlemen on the other side to say what their heated imaginations might suggest, that would seem to be most unequal, as your Lordships determination has gone the whole length, and thereby prevented the defendants from every opportunity of extenuation—certain I am that you will go the whole length also to check the ardour of the gentlemen on the other side It certainly is needless for me to trouble you any more on the particular score of Mr. Bowes, as the observations already mentioned seem to satisfy all alarm that might have been taken up on that occasion. My Lords, to the law on the trial which I had the honor of hearing most satisfactorily laid down by the learned Judge, who tried the cause, I bow with most absolute acquiescence. My Lords, with respect to Mr Bourn, he was taken up after the effect of this conspiracy had taken place, therefore the evidence to affect him is by retrospect, which is an extremely different case, here the evidence being slight in a case where the strongest would be requisite, I trust his case with your Lordships, and no more need be said upon it With respect to Mr. Bowes, although his friends lament we are cut out of all those circumstances that we had made up our minds on, yet there seems to be some circumstances of considerable extenuation indeed, that last circumstance that fell from Mr Chambre is so material, I entreat the particular attention of your Lordship, it seems to me to do away every possible supposition of his intending to make an improper use of the custody of his wife, that is, that he carried her from London to Streatlam castle, where if his behaviour had been of a forcible kind, the probability is, that she would have received some succour. I only beg leave to assume one thing as arising from the affidavits which he has generously and honourably produced, that this stratagem was all his own from the beginning to the end, and he brought all the other parties into it, if that be the case, and there can be no reason why you

should

should suspect it, then the probability will go a considerable length in extenuation of the crime. As to that poor wretch, Prevot, my learned friend has so persuasively entered into his case, that I trust the Court will not punish him, who merely acted under the orders of his master, and followed his steps. With respect to Peacock, the circumstances mentioned by Mr Chambre seem to advert to those disclosed on his own affidavit, which bear the marks of the strongest probability, if it be true that Mr. Bowes did not communicate this to any body. why is he supposed to be privy to it? and there was another circumstance fell from the other side, as to the disguise in which he came to town, and as to the character he assumed, why he assumed it, as he discloses in his affidavit for very different purposes, it certainly will not involve Peacock in any hasty presumption that he was privy to to any design of carrying off Lady Strathmore, I confess, if I am right in my idea, that I should consider alone the public inconvenience sustained by this offence, and that it does not otherwise become very material, and if it is hardly possible for you to shut your eyes altogether against the parties before the Court, yet in what manner can it be allowed to the Gentlemen on the other side, to assume for their client the most unshaken virtue? Will that be allowed to the Gentlemen, while they run contrary to their own sentiments, while they set up a character as unspotted before your Lordships, when they think the truth is against them? The observations Mr. Erskine made on the case, seem to me most peculiarly, indeed, to command your Lordship's attention, what is the duty of a husband? If a husband is involved by means of a wife (I am putting it hypothetically) does it not become the duty of him to seek to recover her from those means? But the present circumstances of the case cut me off from supposing any thing but what the case really was, and Mr. Bowes, who was embracing extreme misery, either by the connivance of those persons about his wife, who had encouraged her to elope, and then were encouraging her to try to rob him of his property, had certainly a right to take care of his wife, but if you had looked a little into the case, you would have seen that the conduct of Mr Bowes would not have led to any suspicion on the part of Lady Strathmore. My Lords, I find that I am not capable of viewing the case with that undisturbed temper of mind that your Lordships possess, and I am sure in the exercise of the most painful part of your duty, your Lordships will regard that which I am sure you will always feel as the highest part of a Judge's character, an inclination to mercy, I am therefore sure your Lordships will attend to all the circumstances that have been urged on the part of these defendants. My Lords, I am now come to that in which I feel a considerable difficulty, namely, in offering to your Lordships an apology for the conduct of Lucas, and, my Lords, I here recur again to the confession of Mr. Bowes, which under the particular circumstances he stands, I am sure the Court will look at with a degree of approbation, the manly and honorable confession of Mr Bowes' that it was all his, and although Lucas surely is to be considered as one of those parties, which Mr Justice Buller said, when his report was read, it is certainly a matter which no man can shut his eyes against, it is impossible to do it away, and yet there are circumstances that will impress themselves, true it is, that Lucas stood in the situation of a peace officer, and that he might regularly expect obedience from every body, but when you consider that Mr Bowes has sworn that he engaged Lucas at first to get the custody of his wife, not informing him of the whole transaction, and that he therefore in order to carry on this design with a certain degree of turpitude annexed to it, but not that degree imputed by the information, he then entered into the design, determined that every stratagem of Mr Bowes to get the custody of his wife should take effect, and in order to do that, he perhaps, in concert with Cummins, hit upon this scheme—that was the probability of it. Now, my Lord, will that be called perjury?—Is there not something in the human mind revolting at the idea of assigning perjury to a case like this?—There was a falsehood about the oath, but what was the purport? [here a loud laugh] My learned friends, I see, are a good deal astonished at the distinction, which I should hardly have taken on another occasion, but was obliged to take it on this—Is every false oath a perjury? —certainly nor—Is there a turpitude to every false oath? Yes. Why is not every false oath perjury?—I answer, the law is a system of wisdom, there may be many kinds of false oaths that are not perjury. Perjury is when it is committed to the injury of a man, and then it is capable of degrees of aggravation, but every perjury ought to be looked at in that point of view—the question is, with what view was it

committed?

committed? Here it is of the most insignificant kind possible, merely to get the footman and the coachman away from the parties, in order to make their scheme successful. Is there any thing in this case that makes one shudder?—because perjury makes an honest man shudder, but, I confess, I do not think there is that about this case which aggravates it so extremely. If, then, the whole design was to put Lady Strathmore into the custody of Mr. Bowes, will you make Lucas, the constable, answer for any of the subsequent conduct of Mr. Bowes? Certainly not—his crime certainly ceases when she was taken. Therefore, this case, which at first sight startled me as subornation of perjury, I confess, on a little consideration, requires more ingenuity than I have in possession to make it out. My Lords, I have nothing more to say,—the Gentlemen on the other side are to answer the affidavits, and to make observations upon them. For myself, I think I may, on the present occasion, appeal to their humanity and candour, which, it seems to me, are more concerned on these occasions than any professional ingenuity whatever.

MR. MINGAY, IN REPLY.

My Lords,

MY learned friend mistook very much both my intention and notion of my situation, if he supposes that I am capable of urging an argument, in a case like this, which requires nothing but the bare state of it, and I should have thought, that before he invoked you to check our ardour, he should at least have controuled his own; he should not have betrayed himself into hypothetical abuses of Lady Strathmore's virtue and character, nor have attempted to have distinguished, in this case at least, between perjury and false swearing: I certainly have no objection to take upon me that character, that Mr Erskine supposes to be the only one that belonged to me, I mean, as counsel for the publick, for in that character alone I shall address myself to you, I shall address to you as placed there to protect that publick, whenever such persons as these defendants dare to violate the laws. The conduct of this prosecution on the behalf of Lady Strathmore has certainly wore a face, through the whole, that cannot prejudice it. I did not offer her as a witness on the trial to violate the feelings of mankind with a narration of those dreadful facts, which she alone is able to set forth, and, therefore, any attack of Mr. Bowes, by insinuation or by evidence, is mean and unmanly; the circumstances he has attempted to introduce have nothing to do with the case in issue before your Lordships, and if he previously knew that, it stamps him as the lowest of men, the evidence he has proposed I had no disposition to keep back from your Lordships' eye, but as counsel for the public (in which character Mr Erskine has thought proper to place me) how would it appear to persons, who by and by search these rolls, to see them so disgraced? and the attempt to do it, is sufficient to shew that the object of Mr. Bowes was to criminate Lady Strathmore, when she, except only as to her personal injury, has not lifted up her voice against him. Have I produced any affidavit at all on the part of Lady Strathmore? or on the part of the prosecution?— Certainly not, and, before I make observations on those that have been produced, I think it incumbent on me to controvert those general arguments that my learned friends have used. There are many persons, of all descriptions, that have their eyes and ears on your Lordships,—are they to go forth and declare to the world, because a man is a servant to a gentleman, he is to aid him in the persecution of a third person? and with respect to Bourn and Provot, that objection goes to them. Why, my Lords, if so, the man that keeps the most servants would be the greatest tyrant. I close the argument by saying, that servants ought to be taught by your Lordships, that, in breaking the laws of their country, whoever teaches them to break those laws, it is certainly penal. But with respect to the duties of a husband, I am sure one of my learned friends cannot speak from his heart—he who adorns that station, as he does every other in which he moves. Why, my Lords, what were the situations of those parties?—Mr Bowes, pretending there was a conspiracy against him,—and that, for the protection of this lady, for the honour of himself, and the children, and for the honour of the family, he is to take her, as he has done, and drag her about the country, as if she was the basest wretch alive! How the Gentlemen can reconcile the evidence on the trial with the duties of a husband, seems to me to be a paradox! My learned friends have said, too, that it became necessary for Mr. Bowes to take the steps he did. Now, only consider for

a moa moment—What was the situation of Lady Strathmore at the time?—There was a suit, which absolutely had been instituted.—If Mr. Bowes had those complaints to make, if he had not treated her in the manner which she charged him with in the Commons, if he was not that adulterer that she charged him with being,—could he not have gone into that court, and tried it in that competent jurisdiction? It is in evidence that he has appealed twice. Has he offered evidence---has he attempted to go there and try the cause as between him and Lady Strathmore? Certainly not. he knew it would be impossible for him to escape. I have a right to say, this verdict finds what his motive was, and if you were to adopt the arguments of my learned friends, you would be converting yourself into a jury to try this cause over again.— Mr Bowes has brought himself into the hardship, and those who have connected themselves with him, I may say, that as they were loving in their lives, I hope in their deaths they will not be divided. If men will join with persons, and trust them, if their lives had been at stake, they must have been forfeited. Suppose Lady Strathmore had been murdered in the heat of this violence,---how would the people concerned have been able to escape? What, by saying, I am a servant, and my master bid me do it! My Lords, I do hope servants will be taught better to-day, and, with respect to the affidavits that have been read before your Lordships, they go this length My Lords, I am counsel on the part of a prosecution, where the persons stands convicted of a conspiracy, and they every one of them swear they did not know what they were doing: if you were to hear these affidavits, why, they are laughing at your Lordships; and the spectators must go out of court, and hold your understandings in contempt----to a degree beyond that in which now every person holds them in admiration Did not Peacock know that he changed his name, and that Bowes wore a great wig, and was watching and dogging particularly the house of Lady Strathmore? and that Lucas should have the audacity to swear here, that he supposed it was because Lady Strathmore had run away with diamonds! I am satisfied you will be of opinion, that in swearing that he is as grossly perjured as Chapman was. Lucas was also the servant of Lady Strathmore, and her protector, in that character Mr. Bowes laid hold of him as a fit person to attend her.— How are these diamonds to be found? The constable knew that a search-warrant was a much better thing. how absurd and farcical it is. Did Lucas take her to find the diamonds in Caen-Wood? Did he take her, expecting to find them at the Bell, at Stilton? How absurd it is for a man to dare to swear those were his motives, when every tittle in the case controverts them, and gives them the lie? That he should insinuate to you, that Lucas entered on such motives as these, must convince you he means to insinuate that which it is impossible he can think you to believe, unless he were an ideot If ten men were convicted of breaking into a house, they will every man swear one for the other, and so will every other set of criminals. Why, look at the circumstances given in evidence, and see whether it is not perfectly clear! This is a work of super-erogation, I have a right to take it for granted that the defendants are all guilty, and the best right in the world, because the jury have found them so, and if you are, after a trial (and such a trial as this too) where, I am sure, no people were more ably defended by the Gentlemen who were separately concerned; and if the jury found their verdict, after no observation on my side, for I had no opportunity of replying, and yet Mr. Chambre says, if you think he ought not to be convicted, you will extenuate the sentence. Why, your Lordships have no right to think about it Why, my Lords, if they meant to move for a new trial, why did they not do it? But they have no right to say there is no evidence against Bourn. As for Mr Thomas Bowes, I really thought it my duty to commend it to Lady Strathmore not to press hard judgment against him for the present, and she, whom these Gentlemen load in this manner with abuse, I am sure, I have found her as complying to every thing that appeared reasonable, in my mind, as any person I ever was conversant with in my life When I was stating to her, that it was possible Mr Thomas Bowes might not have known of that scheme of being ill, and he sent an affidavit, which Lady Strathmore saw, and she said, I leave it wholly to yourself, do it, and welcome I therefore consented not to bring him up now. But, my Lords, with respect to Bourn, he was acting in every part of this scene. Does not he go from place to place? Does not he hear her say—take notice I come here against my will? But, I think, the driver expressly swore, that Mr Bourn came to the door, and that when she went in, she called out, for God's sake recollect I am come here against my will, Bourn says again, but I am servant to Mr. Bowes,—and so he is—

for

for he is an old servant to that family, and has served them many, many years, by which his family, to my knowledge, have been greatly benefitted. With respect to Prevot, I certainly do not wish to point out to you his specifick punishment, it is neither decent nor proper to do it. But, as counsel for that publick, which Mr Erskine has talked of, I entreat you to do it. Lady Strathmore is the party injured,—the laws of the country are violated— and if you send these people away, convicted of a crime, unparalleled in my observation, for I never heard of any thing like it in this great town Here is Mr. Peacock, selected for the purpose of being an acquaintance,—selected, perhaps, by his being eight feet high, and his very appearance, strong, boney, and athletick, as a very proper person to wade through such a scene as this · but he changes his name to Johnson —What for? Why was he to change his name to Johnson? If Mr. Bowes was afraid of his creditors, he was not. My learned friend says, what signifies whether Peacock's name was Peacock, or Johnson. It is evident that Peacock knew that Mr Bowes was about some bad purpose My Lords, why was a poor, harmless, defenceless woman to be thus conspired against? But Mr. Bowes, in this case also, has acted like a ruffian, and if your Lordships do not deter others, by the severity of their punishment, what security have those persons, in whose deaths their husbands have an interest, from committing that crime? But he had no interest in her death,—I am afraid it was nothing else that preserved her life—for he did all but kill her—and then he thrust some gin into her mouth, for the purpose of keeping her alive —Then, why favor these persons who are swearing against one another, and contradicting the verdict of the jury? They have had great indulgence in preferring those affidavits at all. If I had strictly objected, and had stuck close to the rules of law, after conviction of a conspiracy, I take it to be clear law, they have not a right to come and swear they did not commit it?— for if it was so, what a farce it would be— you cannot catch them together,— but if they could come after the verdict, and purge themselves by affidavits, they would, one after another, leave you in the lurch, and leave only one man concerned Mr Fielding says, Mr Bowes has generously taken the whole upon himself It is utterly impossible to say any thing for Mr Bowes—only that he has the character of a husband also—and that aggravates it Are the powers of a husband in this country such, that women that are ill used are not to complain?— Are they so subjected, that she has not as much right to complain as the husband? My Lords, I assert, that Mr. Bowes had no right to have treated Lady Strathmore, in the situation she then was, for any purpose: She was separate from him—there was a suit going on in the Commons—he had no right to take her, even to protect her. If a woman, who is carrying on a suit, is got into the power of her husband again—the law will not permit a woman to be put into that dangerous situation, by which it might all be defeated. With respect to the other persons that have made their affidavits, Susannah Church, Isabel Dixon, and Mary Gowland (or whatever her name is), I have evidence directly contrary to the affidavit she has made. This woman was at Streatlam Castle, in what character, that is not stated to your Lordships, but, I rather suspect, that if Mr Bowes had related her situation, he would not have induced your Lordships to have suspected that he wanted either the comfort or assistance of Lady Strathmore as a wife! But if he picks up these three women, to come and make affidavits of trumpery circumstances, which can be only for the purpose of bewildering your Lordships, and particularly two of your Lordships that were not at the trial,—if you permit these affidavits to be received, they go the length of saying, that these parties are all innocent—for there is no conspiring at all, or, at least, they tell you they do not know it. I do not wonder that the learned Gentlemen have attempted to shelter Mr. Bowes. As to Lucas, they have given him up Lucas knew the coachman and footman——he was the heifer with which they plowed, and they knew all the secrets of the family, by means of which Lucas came into possession of them,—and then, says Lucas, if we can possibly take these two persons, she will be out of protection — I will go up stairs and take her, and then the matter is all done. With respect to Mr. Bowes, why he is waiting to receive these very people at Tottenham Court Road, at the Adam and Eve.— How came he to be placed there, unless he knew of all this? There is Bowes ready to receive her. Under these circumstances, can your Lordships believe that those persons did not all of them know of the purpose of Mr. Bowes?— that he was endeavouring to take Lady Strathmore by force, and to carry her, for the purpose of compelling her to give up that suit! The strong confirmation of the case is—that

Q

he

he had no intereſt in her death. What is his object to make her drop the ſuit?—
Did not he begin it, at Stilton? Obſerve in what way the jury have found him
guilty of theſe circumſtances. Why, it is a paper reſpecting that ſuit. Then again
afterwards it is ſaid, there is no evidence of any perſonal ill uſage of Lady Strathmore. He took care to ill uſe her ſo much in private, he had no occaſion in public,— but it was very proper to know the extent of his ill-uſage. Now, in
order to know that, will your Lordſhips take the evidence of Church, Dixon, and
Gowland, or the evidence of a Gentleman, who is a ſurgeon, who ſaw her at the
moment of her return, at Mr. Farrer's— who tells you ſhe was in a ſtate of great
danger, almoſt frozen to death, with various marks of cruelty and bruiſes. Is this
the way that Mr Bowes thinks Engliſh huſbands are to protect their wives? Is this
the way to conciliate a Lady's affections? Is this the way they are to conciliate the
affections of their families? No man can believe it, and your Lordſhips moſt certainly cannot. However, Mr Bowes wiſhes you to believe, that his object was
merely for the purpoſe of getting Lady Strathmore to be reconciled to him, and to
live together as huſband and wife. It is in evidence before your Lordſhips (to ſhew
the purpoſe of this infamous ſcheme) that he immediately came back to the Commons, and pleaded, that they had lived together from the 12th of November to the
20th---the days of her miſery and perſecution--the days previous to thoſe in which
ſhe appeared to be frozen to death--- he pleaded that they had lived for eight days in
mutual cohabitation and forgiveneſs! Good God — mutual cohabitation and forgiveneſs!——Cohabitation on the mountains in ſnow! I wonder my learned friend
did not check the ardour of Mr Bowes, inſtead of mine. And how the learned
Gentlemen can ſuppoſe their arguments can go down a moment, I cannot deviſe.
When ſhe was brought back, at the end of this amazing forgiveneſs, almoſt frozen
and beat to death, then Mr Bowes has the audacity to go to that very Court, where
before he did not care to ſhew his face, and plead this mutual cohabitation and forgiveneſs! Now, ſays he, I can bring Mary Gowland, who has certainly been in
the ſame ſtate herſelf with Mr Bowes—ſhe, indeed, has lived with him in mutual
cohabitation— for ſhe had juſt had a child by him -----Now, ſays he, I can bring
her to ſwear we were in bed together. Whether, when that poor woman was in
great diſtreſs, Mr Bowes might have laid down by her ſide, I cannot ſay, but
Mary Gowland barely ſwears the fact, without explaining any circumſtance, how
they were in bed together, or any thing of that ſort. The circumſtances, therefore,
that are adduced in mitigation, ſtrike my mind as a great aggravation. But then,
the Gentlemen ſay, they hope you will execute judgment with mercy.—What mercy
has Mr. Bowes ſhewn to Lady Strathmore? I remember once a man, who was ca-
pitally convicted of a moſt barbarous murder, fall on his knees, and ſaid to Mr
Baron Eyre, the Judge who tried him—for God's ſake, my Lord, ſhew me mercy.
—That excellent Judge made the beſt anſwer in the world, and you will make the
ſame to Mr. Bowes—"Man thou has ſhewn no mercy"— This individual criminal
has no right to complain.—What had he who has violated the laws of his country,
—inſulted the perſon of his betters, in every reſpect, except as the law had made
her his wife,— inſulting the publick juſtice of his country in the publick face of
day, at noon-day, in this great town,—and then he is juſt to come and ſay, ſhew me
mercy — You deſerve none, you have ſhewn no regard to the laws of the country
in which you live. It becomes now neceſſary, for the firſt time, for I can find no
ſuch criminals as theſe defendants, therefore you are called upon to day, and I repeat it,—for the firſt time,—to puniſh theſe defendants, convicted of this enormous
crime, to prevent others, by a puniſhment --- the remembrance of which will not
wear off. My Lords, as Mr. Erſkine has denominated me counſel for the publick,
and has choſen to place me in that character, I have no objection to it, but I conſider
myſelf more particularly as counſel for Lady Strathmore, as well as the publick,
and I ſay, that ſhe has been ſcandalouſly abuſed, that ſhe has been inhumanly treated, that Mr. Bowes has forgot all the rights that belonged to a huſband and a
man, and, when you view him in that character—ſhew him what mercy you can.

Mr. Law. My Lords, the learned gentlemen on the other ſide have too well
eſtabliſhed the character of their clients, to make it at all neceſſary for me to preface the
affidavits with which you have been acquainted, and with which the files of your Court
are now diſgraced, if there could have been any thing wanting to compleat this crime,
it would have been the miſerable matter in the affidavits, falſified as it is by the evidence,

dence, and falsified as it is by that indictment from which they fled, when they had assigned as a perjury on the face of that indictment, every one specific fact, and when the proper moment came for deciding that from the testimony of witnesses, they shrunk from that enquiry, therefore I do contend before your Lordships, that every fact that is sworn in the articles of the peace is confirmed conclusively, and I must say, that in the little memory I have of what has ever past in this Court, or of a longer period of time in my memory, and with the assistance of any history I can embrace, there never was an instance in which any criminals convicted really of a misdemeanor, stood before your Lordships for judgement under circumstances of equal aggravation, this I say, whether you contemplate the end, or the means used to obtain it—the end was to make the Lady return to the custody of a husband, who for eight long years had abused the patience of an injured suffering woman—suffering under treatment the most savage—the most brutal What were the first articles of peace in 1785 ? They are upon the records of the Court—I appeal to the Court for the propriety of these observations—I may appeal to every matter of record upon the files of this Court—I say on those articles of 1785, she states herself to have had pins run into her tongue, blood squeezed out of her mouth, ears, and nose——

Mr ERSKINE I object to this Mr Law—I conceive I am at liberty to advert to this, because at the time this injury was done, the articles of the peace were just expired

COURT. We cannot go into that

Mr LAW Then Mr Bowes was just now enlarged from that extraordinary restraint—this was not a sudden gust of passion, it was not an injury done without thought—without premeditation, you find it on the evidence of my Lord's notes, so early as the 14th of October, various conspirators were assembled in disguises, they are collected, and to each is distributed the part that party is to act—they remove themselves to town, after they have acquired one associate, whom they had brought up from Staffordshire, there Mr Bowes prepares them for the hardiest act of violence, they might be required to execute, by carrying them out with arms in coaches, visiting the entries of the metropolis, at last they suppose that their schemes might be rendered abortive, and Mr Bowes then found it necessary to throw before Lady Strathmore some kind of deception, that might dupe the vigilance and suspicion of the most wary, he found it necessary to decamp—on the 23d of October he goes down to Durham, he lays that foolish plan which was executed on the 25th, of falling off his horse, that Lady Strathmore might be seduced from that state of guard and watchfulness which she kept for her protection, in this part of the business Bourn is connected with him, for what purpose could Bourn conceive that Mr Bowes fell from his horse ? his circulating the story of the fall, in hopes of its reaching the ears of a most considerable and most respectable person, if it was not to pave the way for something more material, is ridiculous at this period Bourn is connected—Bourn in the next period receives a letter, he follows them, he tries at the execution of the scheme in town, he makes his appearance at the Castle, and when they get to town their project assumed a a fresh tone and vigour, by the deceptions of Lucas, and as if all cold and indolent before, he aids stratagem by force, he taking advantages from his character as a peace officer of insinuating himself into the Lady's confidence, and duping her more easily Mr. Bowes has chosen to say, that he believed all the time that Lady Strathmore was away from him, that she was pining in some measure for a restoration to his society, that she was set in tears, now this messenger, Mr Lucas, might have learned the true state of her mind, and might have paved the way to a reconciliation but he never founded her sentiments on that subject—in a word, he alarmed her, he received her pay for another person, and having got this entrance into the citadel, it would have been no very difficult thing to have carried her off by force, less criminal than that by which she was carried away, but it seems as if there was a particular constitution in Mr Bowes, he is not satisfied with being a perpetrator of mischief, unless he also is one of the most dangerous disturbers of the public peace, he held out the name of one of the first magistrates—he told her to mitigate her fears, you are going before Lord Mansfield, and by means of a perjury the most unequivocal, capable of being denied, or explained by Cummins, if he had appeared before the Justice, but not explained perjury in an affidavit, in which he states himself to have apprehended violence from Mrs Morgan, and the coachman and footman, all of whom expressly swear the contrary, and that by means of this perjury, and a real and unequivocal subornation of that perjury in Lucas—in Bowes, is this Lady carried away at mid-day,

in

in the moſt public ſtreet, now I cannot fancy to myſelf a more open outrage to the laws of any civilized country, by means of this perjury is Lady Strathmore carried off— But Mr Bowes produces an affidavit which compleats, if any thing was wanting to compleat his guilt, that ſham converſation between Dove and Mr Bowes, and Lucas, in which he ſays, he hopes there is nothing illegal in it My Lords, after this period of time, what this poor woman ſuffered is beſt explained by the articles of peace, and which I do ſay are clearly evidence in this caſe, and deſcribe.

Mr ERSKINE The Court reſolved they ſhould not be referred to.

Mr LAW They reſolved on the articles of peace in 1785, you know ſhe has come twice before this Court, we did not fill up the blank and interval as we might have done, for certainly we thought that fact was ſo filled up, I will not ſtate to your Lord-ſhips any further detail of the circumſtances, except as far as it is impoſſible for you, believing the articles to be true, and the evidence of the ſurgeon and of Mrs Morgan, it is impoſſible to believe one word of what is ſworn of that abominable vivacity, to call it no worſe, with which this Lady is ſuppoſed to be talking of the ſpirits and be-haviour of Mr Bowes—it is indecent, and would diſgrace a brothel, if it was paſted on its walls My Lords, give me leave to aſk in what claſs of crimes is this crime to be ranked? The law books conſider conſpiracies as groſly infamous and ſcandalous, it is ranked with forgery, with perjury, with cheats, to all of which the law annexes in-famous puniſhments—there were five or ſix different defendants in the caſe of the King and Shaw, and they had every one of them a peculiar note of infamy fixed upon them, if the parties guilty of that conſpiracy come with other crimes likewiſe infamous, and draw after them infamous puniſhments, they muſt take the conſequences of their infa-my, as to Lucas's infamy, it is the habit of his life, and if he is raiſed to that bad emi-nence to which all good men wiſh him to be raiſed, it will have no other effect upon him, than only to give him the command of a larger horizon, and enable him to view all the aſſociates of his former life at once, how ſuperior he may be to all the ſhame of ſuch a ſituation, little in his opinion, yet I truſt he is vulnerable to pain and ſenſible of corporal feeling, and ſuch ſort of puniſhments properly belong to ſuch men for ſuch crimes, as to Mr Bowes, what is puniſhing him, but excluding from ſociety thoſe who are already the out-caſts of it, for if a gentleman is introduced into honor-able and liberal company by means of his fortune and education, and will commit ſuch crimes as theſe, he ſhould know that he commits thoſe crimes at the penalty of the ex-cluſion from a ſociety to which he had been introduced—he ſhould know that he com-mits them at the expence of being excluded from every thing that is honorable and worthy, and that will be the beſt puniſhment for him, as to the arguments that have been uſed in mitigation for Bourn and Prevot, that they are ſervants, that they acted under his authority—why, my Lords, the crime of ſervants in no age, and in no com-munity, has ever been held light, if maſters are prevented from committing crimes by means of their ſervants, the miſchief of their own arm would be great indeed, there-fore, it was the policy of another ſtate, they immediately ſeized on the perſons of all the ſlaves on the firſt crime committed by the maſter, and for the diſcovery of that put them to puniſhment, for the policy of all well-governed ſtates is to ſecure the maſter's innocence by his ſervants, and there never was an idea more miſchievous than that which was entertained before the laſt riots, that women and children were to be ſcreened, it was then the wiſdom of thoſe that ſat to adminiſter the laws, to ſelect for puniſhment women and children, that every body might know that neither age nor ſex can avail thoſe that tranſgreſs the laws. My Lords, in forming the judgment you are about to form for the puniſhment of theſe unhappy men, I hope and pray it will have ſuch a ſalutary ſeverity on this occaſion, that by their ſufferings and ſhame, the moſt flagitious and daring may know how dangerous it is to inſult the laws, and there-by may be deterred from the repetition of ſuch offences, and that every perſon who may hear your Lordſhips judgment this day, may hearing it declare, that you are ſen-ſible you are puniſhing a crime which began in perjury, was carried into effect by the moſt extreme cruelty, and at laſt nearly terminated by murder!

Mr. GARROW My Lords, I ariſe only to acquit myſelf of any want of atten-tion to the duty of my ſituation, I ſhould be extremly vain—much vainer than it be-comes me to be, if I could conceive that any thing I have to offer, could aſſiſt the Court in forming that judgment which they are going to pronounce—I will not keep alive any anxious expectation, or prevent the pleaſure the public will receive by poſtponing the judgment, while I make a ſpeech, but as the caſe appears without ex-

ample

ample in the history of this country, so I hope that the people of this country, and who are here to day will see, that the opinion they have entertained of the admirable theory, and the more admirable practice of the laws of England, is well founded.

S E N T E N C E.

Mr Justice Ashurst Andrew Robinson Bowes, Edward Lucas, Francis Peacock, Mark Prevot, and Henry Bourn, you have been severally tried and found guilty on an information which states by way of preamble, that Lady Strathmore lived separate and apart from you Andrew Robinson Bowes her husband, and that she had instituted a suit in the Spiritual Court for a separation for cruelty and adultery, and that you the several defendants entered into confederacy and combination together, to prevent the prosecution of this suit by force and restraint, and to induce her to drop the said suit, and that in prosecution of this purpose, you assaulted her and ill-treated and imprisoned her, and terrified her with threats and menaces, of this crime the Jury have found all you the defendants guilty. The crime of conspiracy is in itself of a secret nature—it cannot be supposed that the parties entering into it should call witnesses to be present at their meetings, and therefore where a number of men act in concert in any illegal purpose, that is evident that all the parties acted in concert to carry that into execution, though they never were all seen together, this was laid down in the case of the Cock-Lane Ghost, and has ever since been recognized as law—such has been the case here, and you have all acted and taken your parts in the scene of villainy that has been carried on. It would be wasting time unnecessarily, for me to recapitulate the evidence, I shall only just take notice of a circumstance or two which has been made use of in argument, to discriminate the case of Bourn, but in the first place, it might be a sufficient answer to that argument to say, that the Jury have found him guilty of a conspiracy, which, if he was not privy to the design that Mr Bowes had in view, the Jury could not properly have found him guilty of it, but notwithstanding Bourn during the whole of this transaction lived in the Bishoprick of Durham, yet it does seem to me, as Justice Buller laid it down at the time of this trial, that he might be involved in the guilt of this transaction, because it is not necessary though the conspiracy was particularly carried on in London and Middlesex—it is not necessary that he should be proved to be in Middlesex at any one of the times—if that should be laid down to be law, you may very well suppose a case ever so criminal, in which no one could be convicted at all—suppose that parties one living in London, one in Middlesex, one in the Borough, and the other in Herts, they never could be tried in such a case as that, though they were all acting in the prosecution of such an illegal act, and each using his endeavour to compleat it, therefore they must all go unpunished, that would be a monstrous position—I look upon it, that though the principal actors in this conspiracy did their parts in the county of Middlesex, yet any person down in the Bishoprick of Durham acting in concert with them, and concerned in their designs, may be convicted also, although in the county of Middlesex Now it has been proved to the satisfaction of the Jury, that Bourn in the first place was privy to Bowes's scheme of feigning that he had tumbled from his horse, and dislocated his shoulder, and broke his ribs, and one must shut one's eyes very much to think Bourn could be so very much imposed upon, as to suppose this was for a very innocent purpose. Besides all that, after he was carrying her away by night, in this concealed place, there he afterwards lends his assistance, when he could not procure chaises, he lends him his horse, to carry her behind him, the Lord knows where. he does not pre-

tend

tend to say he knew, and you must shut your eyes very much to believe he was innocent, therefore, I think, the jury have done perfectly right in involving him in the guilt imputed to the other defendants The crime, therefore, of which you have been found guilty, does appear to be of as atrocious and daring a nature as ever appeared in a Court of Justice. and, had not the facts been made out by the most incontestable proofs, one should hardly have thought, that in a civilized country, governed by such laws, any set of men would have been found hardy enough to take away a Lady of rank and fortune, from one of the most publick streets of this great town, at mid day, in defiance of all law, order, and government, and to drag her through the heart of the kingdom 240 miles, and, what is a high aggravation of this offence is, that it was meant and intended to impede the current of publick justice, and by force and violence to put a stop to a prosecution legally instituted by her against you, for cruelty and adultery, and in order to effect this wicked purpose, you have corrupted a man of the name of Lucas, whose duty it was to preserve the peace—you have induced him to become the violater of it. As to suborning Chapman to swear against the coachman and footman, that you have, in some degree, exculpated yourself from, it may be you did not tell him to do this act, but when you told him, he must by any means take her person, you could not suppose he would be very delicate about the means, therefore, you, by the first illegal act, make yourself responsible for every thing that followed in consequence of it One should have hoped that you, who have had the advantages of birth, and fortune, and education, would have been superior to such base practices, but you have made use of fortune to corrupt men of lower extraction ·— This has not been the start of sudden resentment, but a cool, deliberate purpose of malice, carried on for a month, at least, for it does appear by that affidavit you have now made, under the pretence of extenuating your crime, that you have harboured this in your mind a much longer time, for you there confess, that you waited only for the time that your recognizances were out, and your sureties discharged, therefore your own affidavit gives judgment against you If that fact, you was about to commit, was innocent, why wait for the time that the sureties for the peace were discharged?—therefore you give judgment against yourself, and shew that you knew the act you was about to perpetrate was illegal, and, in truth, no man in this country can be so ignorant, as not to know it was illegal in the highest degree. But though you was the original contriver of this scene of outrage, and therefore stand more criminally guilty, yet there are other persons that stand highly guilty also —— You, Edward Lucas, you knew it was your business to preserve, and not break the peace, yet you have been guilty of the most daring violation of it, and that under the colour and shelter of your office, for you pretended that you had a warrant against Lady Strathmore, which was totally without all foundation, you have added to the breach of your duty, the crime of treachery, as you was placed about her person as a guard, and was paid for being her protector. As to the under actors, though they are less criminal, yet some of them are very highly reprehensible—particularly you, Francis Peacock, for it does appear that you are a man of fortune, a man of some education, therefore you certainly must, or ought to have known better, and that such a thing as this was not to be tolerated in a country governed by law,— you pretend you did not know what Mr Bowes's intention was, at the time you accompanied him to London,—it is very hard to bring ones-self to believe that you did not know that Mr Bowes was proceeding on some illegal purpose, when he was forced to make use of these circumstances of secrecy and disguise, for fear of being discovered. and it appears, from your own confession, that the morning of this outrage, you did know the purpose of his intention, and that he was going to seize the person of Lady Strathmore by force, and to carry her from this city,—if you knew that, even on the morning, ought not you, or ought not any man, that calls himself a Gentleman, that calls himself an honest man, to have lent his assistance to prevent such a scene of outrage and violence? If you admit that, knowing what his purpose was, you did join him in the prosecution of that illegal intent, and that you did accompany him as far as Stamford, to which place she was carried while you was in his company, it is utterly impossible that you did not know that this was against Lady Strathmore's consent, for it has been proved by a number of witnesses, and, might I suppose, by hundreds more, that in many places she cried out murder, and that she was carried off by force and

vio-

violence. As for the rest of these defendants, though only in the capacity of servants, yet every man, and particularly servants, ought to know, it is no part of their service to enlist themselves into the illegal concerns of their masters—they are only to obey him in all his lawful commands, therefore that service is no kind of excuse for the part you have taken in this business. The Court has taken into consideration the different degrees of malignity attending your several cases, D O T H S E N T E N C E A N D A D J U D G E, that you, Andrew Robinson Bowes do pay a fine of three hundred pounds to the King, and be imprisoned in the custody of the Marshal for the space of three years, and that you do after the expiration of those three years, give security for your good behaviour for the space of fourteen years, commencing from and after the expiration of the said term of three years, yourself in ten thousand pounds, and two sureties in five thousand pounds each, and that you now be remanded to the custody of the Marshal, in execution of this judgement, and until you shall have paid the fine, and that you Edward Lucas, do pay a fine of fifty pounds to the King, and be imprisoned in his Majesty's goal of Newgate for the space of three years, and until that fine be paid, and that you Mark Prevot be imprisoned in his Majesty's goal of Newgate for the term of one year; and that you Francis Peacock do pay a fine of one hundred pounds to the King, and be imprisoned for the space of two years in the custody of the Marshal of this Court, and until that fine be paid, and that you Henry Bourn do pay a fine to the King of fifty pounds, and be imprisoned in the said goal of Newgate for the term of six months, and until that fine be paid.

F I N I S.

CPSIA information can be obtained
at www.ICGtesting.com
Printed in the USA
BVHW022242291222
655301BV00006B/154

9 781275 110311